Ministry Matters

On Shepherding & Finishing Well

Richard I. Gregory

FOREWORD BY RICHARD W. GREGORY

CreateSpace, Charleston, SC

2013

Ministry Matters
On Shepherding and Finishing Well

Copyright 18264-2013 by Richard I Gregory

Printed by CreateSpace, An Amazon.com Company

To order copies of this book by telephone

Call - 863-838-4240

Primarily Scripture is taken from the King James Bible.

Cover Design by Jim Connelly Studio

ISBN: 1483998398

ISBN 13: 9781483998398

Printed in United States of America

Dedication

This book is dedicated to my family, my ministry team. I am especially thankful for Carol, my wife of 57 years, who encouraged me and helped me during the writing of the manuscript and who has provided tender loving care through the years and especially during the time of my illness. My children Debra Ann, Richard William, Jan Carole and Cynthia Lynn have been an integral part of my ministry and have been the source of great joy to their parents..

"I have no greater joy than to hear that my children walk in the truth"
III John 4

The family grew and now it numbers 41. We prayed for those that our children would marry and the Lord graciously answered our prayer. All four married vibrant Christians and are actively serving the Lord in their local churches.

TO MY WIFE, CAROL:

She has faithfully served at my side for over 57 years of ministry. We have prayed together, cried together and rejoiced together. She is a faithful wife, mother, mother-in-law, grandmother and great grandmother. Indeed, she is God's gift to me and our family.

TO THE FAMILY OF DEBRA AND STEVE LOVE:

- James and Mary Love and their children Amelia and Adelaide
- Courtney and Jim Mahon and their children Connor, Vale and unborn child
- Trevor and Kati Love and unborn child

TO THE FAMILY OF RICHARD AND PATRICIA GREGORY:

- Richard and Michelle and their child Emma
- Lauren and Ryan Hougham and their children Brennan and Makenzie
- Abbi, Suzanna and William

TO THE FAMILY OF JAN AND REGGIE KIMBRO:

- Jessica and Tim Davis and their children, Kyle, Kimber and unborn child
- Keri and Nathan Leatherwood
- Erin

TO THE FAMILY OF CYNTHIA AND TIM BULLOCK:

- Josalyn, Kayla, Lindsay and Drew.

These are our family to whom I dedicate this book. It includes 15 grandchildren and their spouses and 9 precious great grand-children. We are thankful to the Lord for allowing us to live to see them as vibrant Christians. May all that come behind us be found faithful.

"Children's children are the crown of old men, and the glory of children are their fathers" **Proverbs 17:6**

Acknowledgements

Carol Ann Gregory – my helpmeet and partner
in ministry, for her insightful suggestions, patient
encouragement and faithful support and prayers,
during the process of creating the manuscript.

Dr. Richard W. Gregory – for his persistent encouragement
to write this book and his help in editing of the manuscript.

Patricia Gregory - for her constant availability for medical
guidance and counsel since the beginning of my illness.

Richard P. and Michelle Gregory – for their help in formatting
the manuscript and for their participation in its editing.

Reggie and Jan Kimbro – for their tender loving
care for us and their provision of a quiet home
enabling me to finish the manuscript.

Steve and Debra Love – for being the first of my family to urge
me to write and for being there whenever we had a need.

Tim and Cynthia Bullock – whose constant concern
for our welfare was a great encouragement.

Rev. Paul Seger and Dr. Robert Provost – my co-workers
in Missions, who urged me to write my experiences
as a resource for pastors, spiritual leaders
and the body of believers.

Jim Connelly – of Jim Connelly Studios, for his generous and creative design of the book's cover.

Keri McLaughlin – for the cover photo of the author. Lastly, for the many family and friends who prayed for me and thus sustaining me with strength and focus during the time of the writing of this manuscript.

Contents

Foreword

T he most valuable seats at an important event
are the ones in the front row. It seems that
courtside tickets to the NBA or dugout tickets
for the MLB – despite exorbitant costs – are sold-out
for every game! Everyone with the means attempts to
get the best seats that they can. Those seats are the
ones that allow the greatest "experience" – the sights,
sounds, and smells are so dynamic that it feels like you
are actually part of the action.

I grew up in a pastor's home with a front row seat
every day. I saw the truth lived out, heard the truth
told out, smelled the fragrances of ministry in such
a dynamic way that I was indeed part of the action
of watching a servant of Christ being used by Christ
to build the church of Christ. I saw the grief, tedium,
routines, defeats, and discouragements, as well as the
joys, victories, privileges, and delights served up at
times within one day! I saw the tremendous stability
that the grace of God affords a pastor who sincerely
loves Christ. The sense of deep appreciation and awe

at Christ's love and grace seemed to perpetually fill the air, filling our spirits with awareness that life itself depended upon that love and grace.

We were taught in our home that in order to enjoy the blessings of God in the future days, we needed to delight in the blessings of God today. Living for Christ became the natural desire in light of Christ dying for us. The more Christ's work of redemption was high-lighted, the less hesitation existed to live for Him. In fact, "living for Jesus" was the expectation in light of the Gospel – not as a means of merit, but as a means of reflecting His life and the power of God's love. We were repeatedly oriented that my parents weren't as concerned about sin in our lives as they were about the presence of Christ in our lives. Faithfulness to Christ was the standard set by the head of our home – whether it was in the public venues at church or the privacy of our family away on vacation. He was the same guy – seeking to remain faithful and to honor the Lord in the way that he lived.

As he matured as a leader, my father grew to recognize that faltering was a possibility at any time without the ever-abiding reliance upon the grace of God. His great concern was that none of the glories of Christ that had been manifested in his earlier minis-try be discredited by a lapse during his later ministry. He became fixed on seeing Jesus magnified to the very end. Ministry matters to him until the very last moment that God blesses him with the ability to serve. Finishing well is his criterion for his entire ministry.

In a day when many in the church ignore the riches available in highly esteeming our spiritual heritage, we need to hear from men who have demonstrated the value of faithfulness to the Lord throughout 50 years of ministry. Such faithfulness to the Lord is truly what makes ministry matter. The practical wisdom shared throughout this book will serve younger pastors well. The unique mixture of biblical insights, practical experience, theological awareness, and emotional stability will stimulate an aspiration for even greater faithfulness regardless of a man's maturity in ministry. Your seat, as you read this book, may not be in the front row, but it'll be a great seat!

Rick Gregory
Senior Pastor – Grace Bible Church
Fair Oaks, California

"The things that you have heard of me among many witnesses, commit thou to faithful men who shall be able to teach others also." 2 Timothy 2:2

Introduction

I looked out the picture window at the softly fall-
ing snow as it covered the valley below. Carol
and I were in our last month as a pastoral team
in Honesdale, Pennsylvania. This particular stop had
been a wonderful experience. I had "retired" several
times before, but every time the Lord was gracious
to bring a number of interim ministry opportunities
into my life. Each of these heaped further blessing
onto what was already a joyful ministry career. Finally,
when approached about coming home to serve as
interim pastor of the church where I grew up, an affir-
mative decision was immediate. Now after more than
two and half years, our time there was nearly complete. The snow was making this particular weekend
difficult. We were in the midst of our Annual Missions
Conference and it looked like the Saturday night
meeting was going to be "snowed out." Having grown
up in that Pennsylvania valley, I knew fourteen inches
of snow on Halloween weekend was certainly abnor-
mal. Paul Seger, General Director of Biblical Ministries

Worldwide, and a treasured ministry partner, was the speaker for our conference and was staying with us. Being snowed in gave us some very precious time together.

We talked about a wide range of subjects, but the one that dominated our time was the alarming casualty rate among today's pastors. Paul asked me to share with him how I survived as a pastor, and what insights from my experience I would pass on to younger men. Over a cup of coffee on that cold afternoon, I spoke to my friend of biblical principles that had been mined in the study, forged on the anvil of experience, and proven on the field of ministry. At every turn the Lord reinforced these principles through the ups and downs of a life spent in ministry. Paul said to me "Men who finish well are rare. The young men just starting out in ministry are not hearing these very practical insights that the Lord has taught you." Seger's challenge immediately brought to mind a text penned by his namesake – the Apostle Paul – over 2,000 years ago. In 2 Timothy 2:2 the great pastor, evangelist, and missionary said at the conclusion of a faithful ministry, *"the things which you have heard from me in the presence of many witnesses, entrust these to faithful men who will be able to teach others also."*

I knew then that if I were to be faithful to this command, I must record the numerous lessons that the Lord taught to me in the past six decades. After my last retirement, the diagnosis of a terminal illness made it clear that this was to be my final retirement. As I found myself looking for a way to continue productively serving the Lord, I was continually reminded by the Lord through the mouths of those closest to me: "You can still write. You *need* to write."

And so I am. I have agreed to give it a try in the work that you are now holding. My intention is not to produce a comprehensive encyclopedia of how to do ministry, but simply to replicate that conversation on a snowy afternoon. This book seeks to answer the ultimate question: "How do I finish well?" The answer is mercifully simple, and yet painfully complicated. The way to cross the line victoriously in ministry is to unswervingly seek out and apply biblical principles to your life as you seek above all else the glory of Christ. That's the simple truth. But it's here where the complexity enters. Life is complex. Ministry is complicated. People are diverse. It's easy to answer the question simply, but the application of biblical principles in varied contexts becomes far more challenging.

Towards that end, in this book, I have addressed a variety of pastoral insights that the Lord has taught me over the years. My goal is to simply state these principles in a series of brief talks on a variety of subjects. I do not hold up the anecdotes that I give as illustrations of these truths as the perfect model for pastoral ministry. It is merely the record of how the Lord taught me these things, and how I applied the principles in the context where the Lord placed me. These are the experiences that the Lord used in my life to mold me into the man of His design. I am also aware that from time to time I was not the most cooperative piece of clay, and on numerous occasions resisted the hand of the Potter. In spite of this the Lord was gracious to me, to spare me from great shattering.

Many of these talks are well known principles practiced by many. Over the years, my concern has been that many spiritual leaders do all the right things but at times with the wrong attitudes and hidden motives. I shall attempt to harmonize these so that the result is a description of servant leadership that is spiritual, courageous, discerning and caring.

It is my intention in the following chapters to address a number of the lessons learned in my years as a Christian, Pastor, Member of several Mission and Seminary Boards, Overseer of a Fellowship of Churches, Parent, Husband and Grandfather. The ministry to which the Lord called me enabled me to travel around the world, to minister in a variety of cultures, pastor small, middle size and large churches.

Preaching has always been my singular passion but today's spiritual leader is called upon to be so much more. This often takes a man into uncharted waters where the potential for mistakes is so much greater. My journey includes successes and abundant rejoicing, but is also marked by mistakes, humiliations, failures and heartaches. Even in all these we are more than conquerors through the Lordship of Jesus Christ. We learned to receive from the Lord's hand whatever He planned for us. We know God works together in all things to bring to pass our conformity to His Son, Jesus Christ.

"The things that you have heard of me among many witnesses, commit thou to faithful men who shall be able to teach others also." 2 Timothy 2:2

CHAPTER ONE

Is the Call of God Important in Spiritual Leadership?

One afternoon a young man came into my study to talk about becoming a missionary. A number of years earlier, he had spent a summer in South America on a student mission trip with our church young people. When he returned there was no evidence that the trip had impacted his interest in missions. Now he was entertaining the possibility of returning there as a missionary. Since his involvement in our local church missions program was nominal, I decided to pointedly ask him why he felt that the Lord wanted him to become a missionary. I was taken back by his answer. He stated that his present vocation did not afford him enough time as he would like to spend with his children. He had observed that the missionaries he visited had much more time with their families than he did and therefore becoming a missionary would enable him to do a better job raising his children. Needless to say, we did not pursue him as a viable missionary candidate from our church. Understanding the call of God is the jumping off point for ministry.

ON UNDERSTANDING THE CALL OF GOD

There is much confusion today about what constitutes the Call of God as to whether it is to a vocation, a mission field, a pastorate or a variety of other Christian ministries. What is the call of God to ministry? Is there a call of God to ministry? A few years ago a book about decision making and the will of God suggested that God does not have a particular will apart from the direct instructions in the Word of God. If God does not directly instruct in the Scriptures, then one is free to choose whatever he desires. According to this deistic approach, God's will does not include a particular person to be your wife or husband; He does not call any to a specific ministry or mission.

This perspective results in the belief that no one has a call from God. Everyone is thus free to experiment with a variety of choices as long as he stays within the bounds of Scripture. According to this view, David, Isaiah, Jeremiah and Paul cannot be considered as normative for the purpose of illustrating the reality of the call. Thus, there is no call of God upon the life of a man to ministry.

I think it becomes evident that our God does place His hand on certain of His servants for specific ministry and function in the church whether it be as a missionary, pastor, teacher, elder, deacon or any other ministry that demands one's full life focus. The question is often asked, "How can I be certain that I have been called of the Lord?" While serving on a mission board, I addressed this subject in a prefield orientation session, and was surprised to find numerous candidates with no assurance that "their choice" to be a missionary was due to the call of God upon their lives.

Many believe that vocational ministry is a matter of choice. This was reinforced for me while interviewing a young man for ordination. I asked if he found the ministry to be too demanding on his family, what would he do? His answer reflected the view that ministry is a matter of choice when he said, "I would seek to find another vocation that fit my talents."

In recent years, I have found that the concept of a "call" to ministry (along with its lifelong commitment) has fallen on hard times. Perhaps it is because we have spoken of the "call" in such mystical terms that require some puncticular experience to validate its authenticity. Or perhaps it is because our faith has become so man centered that we have "put" ourselves in the ministry and can remove ourselves at will.

We did not put ourselves into the ministry, and must be careful of taking action that would remove us from the ministry to which God has called us. This is the work of God, and as such it is a serious business that must not be viewed lightly or claimed whimsically. As the brother of Jesus says in James, *"Let not many of you become teachers, my brethren, knowing that as such we will incur a stricter judgment."* The man who understands the call of God understands the soberness of spirit that must accompany him.

This was a heavy burden on my heart for I had an awesome understanding of the serious nature of handling the Word of God. I remember one morning when I retired to a garden in back of the Administration building at Shelton College. In my prayer time I told the Lord that I never wanted to preach error and if I ever did, I asked the Lord to take me home before I polluted the church with false doctrine. Some have said that I was young and foolish, but I was deadly serious, and expected God to grant that request. Needless to say, it made me very careful of what I preached.

ON INTERPRETING THE CALL

Interpreting the call requires the evaluation of desire, current obedience, external testimony and biblical qualification. I do believe choice is involved in this concept of God's call. One must choose to live in such a way that he can hear and respond to the call of God to ministry and at times to specific locations in which to exercise that ministry. This is based upon the biblical teaching that as a believer I have been purchased by the blood of Christ, and therefore am no longer on my own to make my own decisions apart from my Master's involvement. I am subject to a sovereign Lord's approval in all areas of my life. Paul says in 1 Thessalonians 2:4 *"But as we were allowed of God (tested and found faithful) to be put in trust with the gospel, even so we speak: not as pleasing men, but God which trieth our hearts."*

In saving me to serve Him, He also specifically gifted me for that service. Whether or not I am in vocational ministry, I am responsible to utilize my spiritual giftedness within the life of the church. The Bible gives ample reason to believe that the Lord sovereignly reaches into the affairs of men and designates certain of His servants to carry out specific ministries designed to fulfill His purposes for His church. Ministries like the pastor-teacher and evangelist mentioned in Ephesians 4:11 are good illustrations of this.

God is finished with His audible communication and therefore it is senseless to look for some kind of voice or even visual sign in determining the call of God. In our day, God speaks to His servants by the Holy Spirit's illumination of the Scriptures. If one is to find a message from God in life's circumstances he must look beyond incidents, and find out how his spiritual priorities fit the messages God has already revealed in His Word. As one consistently reads His Word he will find that 95% of God's will for him is clearly found in its instruction. When one's spiritual priorities are consistent with God's Word, the Holy Spirit moves to provide a burden and a pervasive inner desire for a particular ministry. As Paul says in I Timothy 3:1, *"If a man desires the office of overseer, it is a fine work he desires to do."*

Involvement in that sphere of ministry provides the resources needed for others to reinforce the Holy Spirit's leading in our lives. It is the "law of two witnesses." Someone once said, "All I can be is willing, others must determine my worthiness." That is why men were appointed or ordained to ministries and missionaries are commissioned. The call of God is constituted by the witness of the Holy Spirit with one's inner spirit and the affirmation in one's life by others. It is that hunger and thirst to be involved in a particular ministry where one's gifts are utilized and one's training is maximized coupled with the appointment of others that verify this responsibility.

The man who would know if he is called, must first ask whether he is burdened, obedient, confirmed, and qualified. These were the issues that I was forced to grapple with as a young man. I can still recall spending time on my knees, pouring my heart out to God until late in the night, struggling with my willingness to surrender my life to a life of missions in Africa. When I finally came to the place where I said to the Lord, "Lord, whatever you want to do with my life, I want to be willing" a peace swept over my soul. Although Africa was not God's will for my life, being willing to surrender to whatever the Lord wanted was the real issue. This was not the only incident that confirmed the call of God on my life.

ON THE BIBLICAL EVIDENCE FOR THE CALL

When Paul spoke to the elders at Ephesus, he emphasized that they had been "set" as overseers by the independent action of the Holy Spirit. He chose the aorist middle indicative of the verb *tithami* which means "to put, place or set." Paul chooses this word to describe what God did for him in "putting him into the ministry" (I Timothy 1:12). In both Ephesians and I Timothy, he uses this aorist middle voice indicating that the action was performed by God himself independently of the choice of men.

In Scripture, numerous men are placed as overseers over the Lord's flock independently of their own choice. In Paul's case, God appointed him as an apostle prepared to be the Lord's servant. Clearly, men in

Scripture received a call from God to a specific ministry. Paul further describes the character of his calling in his testimony before King Agrippa. He quotes the words of the Lord when extending his call to go to the Gentiles. Even in this instance, he chose the aorist middle of the verb *procheirizo* - meaning to appoint beforehand - indicating that the Lord had determined this choice for Paul apart from Paul's cooperation.

It is very obvious that God was very purposeful in calling the Apostles. In the case of Peter and Paul He even designated the people upon whom they should focus the conduct of their ministry. Luke records for us the message given to a concerned Ananias about Paul. *"Go thy way for he is a chosen vessel unto Me, to bear My name before the gentiles, and Kings and the children of Israel."* Paul had an understanding of this and opens most of his epistles with reference to the fact that he is "called to be an Apostle" or is an Apostle by the will or commandment of God. He further communicates to Timothy that he knows that the Lord "put" him in the ministry despite his sordid history. He chooses to use a Greek word that means "to appoint or to place."

The biblical narrative employs the concept of sovereign design in describing the placement of certain individuals in particular offices and ministries. In the case of Jeremiah, the Lord says that He chose the prophet before he was ordained as a prophet, or even conceived in his mother's womb (Jeremiah 1:5). The Lord pointed out to David that He had taken him out of the sheepcote and made him King over Israel (2 Samuel 7:8). In all these instances, the calling was the Lord's doing. Rather than making a man proud, it should be a source of great humility and fear. It does indicate that the Lord's plan includes specific individuals that He calls to fulfill His designs.

There were numerous other examples of this concept in Scripture. The writer of Hebrews in commenting on the office of High Priest states *"no man taketh this honor unto himself, but he that is called of God, as was Aaron"* (Hebrews 5:4). Some will say that these circumstances were unusual and should not be considered the norm, yet the New Testament teaches us that in order for the church to function as God intended, these kind of appointments had to be made (Acts 14:23). It is here recorded that men were *"appointed as elders."* In Titus 1:5 Paul writes *"For this cause left I thee in Crete, that thou shouldest set in order the things that are wanting, and ordain elders in every city."* In Acts 20:28 where the terms overseer, elder and pastor are used interchangeably, it should be noted that men are placed (made) in these offices and functions by the Holy Spirit. This seems to indicate cooperation in this process between God and men. The word translated "made" in this verse is the same word Paul used of himself when he said that the Lord had "put" him in the ministry.

The final and greatest biblical proof for the concept of a "call" towards men is the effectual call of God to salvation. The call of God to salvation is the result of His sovereign grace, and is directed at individuals whose names are written in the Lamb's Book of Life before the foundation of the world. The call of God to ministry is also directed at individuals whose lives are planned out for them by a sovereign God that involves himself in their lives bringing to pass His will.

It is a fearful thing to realize that the Lord has placed His hand on a man with the intent that **he** will accomplish for Him service for the Kingdom. Without that realization, our service can be characterized by selfish desire and personal promotion rather than seeking the glory and honor of the One who called him.

ON FACING UNCERTAINTY

We faced this in the process the Lord used to bring us to Limerick Chapel. Carol and I were with our young people at Harvey Cedars Bible Conference when a dear lady from Memphis, Tennessee asked me if I would be interested in having my name presented to the pulpit committee at her church. I replied that we were very happy and content in our present ministry and had no interest in moving. Her answer to me was a bit unnerving. She pointed out that possibly we were so content that we would not hear if the Lord was speaking to us. That afternoon, on the beach, Carol and I talked about our conversation and we concluded that the Lord had given us no indication that a move to a new ministry was a part of His will. I returned home that night and when I went to the post office there were three letters from churches asking if I were interested in being a potential candidate. It was like a wakeup call from the Lord. We examined the material from all three churches and decided that the material from a Church in Indiana was most compatible with our doctrinal and ministry philosophy. I wrote the church and said that I can't say I am interested and I can't say that I am not. I received a telephone call from the church asking that I come out to preach. Looking at my schedule, I told the church that I could not come until the first week in October and since this was August, I didn't know if the church could wait that long. They said that they could wait and we scheduled a Wednesday through Sunday in October. We had a wonderful time and we felt that the church would vote to call us but underneath we were disquieted and unsure. We still had no desire to leave the ministry at the Braintrim Baptist Church in Laceyville. Driving home, we stayed that night at a motel in Bedford, Pennsylvania and spent a good in Laceyville agreeing to pray together about such a move. The Board of Deacons issued an invitation to come and preach and after preaching, the Deacons voted to make me a candidate. The longer the process took, the more fearful we became. We struggled with thoughts of failure and the magnitude of the responsibility, but decided that we would ask the Lord for a 90% vote to give us the confidence that He was indeed leading. The church voted by mail with each member receiving a ballot. Missionaries had the opportunity to designate the Board to vote a proxy vote. In the end, we received a 99% vote and accepted the call with dependence upon the Lord.

In this process, we faced fear, failure, uncertainty and other factors that needed the sustaining grace of God. We claimed the promise of sufficient grace that where God calls He sustains, provides, protects and enables.

ON THE IMPORTANCE OF THE CALL

It is the assurance that one has a call from God that keeps an individual in ministry. The longer one functions within the framework of the calling of God the more assured one becomes of the sovereign hand of God in choosing both the ministry and the sphere where that ministry is exercised. When the way gets rough and discouragement is present, the knowledge of the call of God upon one's life keeps one from quitting.

Recently I was talking to a mission executive. He said, "I can't even envision spending my life doing anything other than what I am doing." Another man in the room commented, "that is because God has called you to this ministry." That man had an understanding of the effects of the biblical "call of God." Without this understanding, ministry is simply a choice to be entered and left according to the circumstances that life dictates. With this understanding, one perseveres even when discouraged and disappointed with people, circumstances and unfulfilled expectations because he is confident that he has been called of God.

Paul lists those things that happened to him in 2 Corinthians 4:8-18 concluding that the trials of this life are temporary but the rewards of faithful service are eternal. Luke in recording the occasion of Paul's conversion in Acts 9:15-16 quotes what the Lord said to a concerned Ananias: *"Go thy way: for he is a chosen vessel unto Me, to bear My name before the Gentiles and kings, and the children of Israel; For I will show him how great things he must suffer for My name's sake."* This caused Paul to share with the Ephesians Elders: *"And now, behold, I go bound in the spirit unto Jerusalem, not knowing the things that shall befall me there: Save that the Holy Ghost witnesses in every city, saying that bonds and afflictions abide in me. But none of these things move me, neither count I my life dear unto myself, so that I might finish my course with joy, and the ministry that I have received of the Lord Jesus, to testify the gospel of the grace of God"* (Acts 20:22-24).

CHAPTER TWO

How Do I Build My Family into a Ministry Team?

After five years of ministering elsewhere, we received an invitation to return to the church for a Sunday, and we brought our youngest daughter with us. I had spent seventeen years as its pastor. We were invited back to the parsonage for dinner and a time of fellowship with the present pastor. While there, the pastor's wife asked our daughter about the secret that caused so many people to love the "Gregory children." Our daughter shared that when she came into the foyer on that very morning she saw a group of her friends, and started toward them when suddenly she remembered the widows on the Deacon's Bench. Rather than join her friends, she remembered her former ministry from years ago, and went over to the widows giving each a hug and spending a few minutes sharing with them before joining her friends. Participation in ministry was the answer to the question. In my own mind this underscored the importance of viewing the pastor's family as a key component in his ministry.

ON THE PASTOR'S CHILDREN

A pastor's children must be taught that they are in his family by design not default. If we believe in the call of God "putting a man in the ministry" then the wife and children God gives to him are an integral part of that ministry. It is very important that this concept be understood by a pastor's children. By design, our children were important members of our family ministering team and so I included them whenever it was appropriate.

One of the ways we accomplished this was to assign ministry tasks to our children each Lord's Day. As mentioned previously, we involved our children in ministry by suggesting to them responsibilities suited to their age. We shared with the children the importance of helping to meet the needs of the elderly who are often very lonely. Each Sunday morning the children would make it a priority to talk to the elderly ladies who often sat on several deacon's benches in the foyer. We discussed with them their ministry opportunities at our Sunday dinner. An additional opportunity for service, the children were given the responsibility of seeing to it that the pencils in the pew backs were sharpened and ready to use. Since our church was some forty pews deep, it was a significant time consumer each week. As our children grew, their involvement in ministry expanded beyond the sharpening of pencils but visiting the elderly always remained important. When my son was old enough, I would take him along with me on my pastoral visitation. When they were teenagers, they served as a part of our summer ministry teams that conducted Bible clubs all across our area.

Carol and I made a concerted effort to point out all of the benefits being a pastor brought to our family. We shared prayer requests and their answers as we rejoiced together when we were able to observe the Lord's work in hearts and lives. They soon began to understand that being in ministry was not a "job," but a privileged responsibility with eternal dividends.

The influence of the oldest child upon her siblings is of utmost importance. Our oldest, Debra, had a spiritual depth that included a consistent testimony. She regularly had her personal devotions and memorized chapters of the Word of God. Her testimony in her public school often brought ridicule and persecution. She never wavered in her devotion to Christ. Being the oldest, the other children looked up to her and her influence upon them was of great value in those formative years.

Today, all of our children are deeply involved in their churches, with a love for serving Christ. Our eldest is an elder's wife, our son is a pastor, our third child is a pastor's wife and our youngest is a teacher in a Christian school. Their preparation for service to the Lord began as "preacher's kids" with a mother that carefully guided the attitudes of her children toward God's family, the church, and the ministry our family had been given.

ON THE PASTOR'S WIFE - A GIFT FROM THE LORD

Carol and I were teenage sweethearts. I met her the summer of my junior year in high school and our relationship developed through church activities and involvement in her father's evangelistic meetings. She had a profound effect on my spiritual growth and I credit her for challenging me to begin a walk with the Lord that would demonstrate the seriousness of my faith to my classmates. The groundwork was laid during those years of "courting" for a ministry partnership in the years to come. I have always considered her to be a gift from God specifically designed to be a help meet for the ministry God would give me. Her gifts and disposition compliment the areas where I did not excel.

A pastor's wife creates and promotes the attitudes that control the home and frame the development of a family ministering team. An effective husband-wife team must share a similarly intense love for the people in the flock. If the pastor's wife does not love the flock the Lord has entrusted to her husband, there is a great danger that she and her children could end up with tremendous bitterness and resentment.

The involvement of the pastor's wife needs to be balanced in her ministry. Many times the pastor's wife (and even the pastor himself) involves herself in ministry so deeply that the family relationships are neglected. This is an extreme, since the wife's involvement in ministry should always be primarily one of ministry to her husband and family. The opposite extreme is equally damaging where the wife is entirely disconnected from her husband's ministry to the church. Where the pastor is called of God to the ministry, the pastor's wife is called by God to be his helper both within and without the home.

The time she dedicates to ministry in the life of the church must be predicated upon the stages of life in the development of her family. There are lengthy periods of time in the life of a woman where her primary focus, by default, must be the home. She must recognize this as her highest calling, for without a home that is decent and in order, the pastor loses credibility as a spiritual leader. A pastor's family must be paramount to him, and he must never neglect his ministry to his wife and children. Indeed, his wife and children must be primary in his ministry. They should never be considered apart from his ministry, but as an integral part of ministry itself. According to the Apostle Paul in 1 Timothy 3:4-5 failure to have a wife and children that are willing to follow a pastor's spiritual leadership disqualifies a man from ministry as an elder.

The pastor's wife has a tremendous ability to bless the church by releasing her husband to do the work of the ministry. The wife who resents the time her husband spends in ministry presents a tremendous danger. In such cases a wife will consider the ministry a burden and may even withdraw from being her husband's ministry partner. Ultimately the wife with this perspective will undermine the attitudes of her family toward the church. Attitudes are caught not taught. So often I hear of preacher's kids rebelling and turning away from the Lord. While there is no easy reason for this, and while every situation is unique, the application of some very basic principles can help to avoid such tragedies. There are a number of ways that undermining, critical attitudes can be present in a pastor's home.

ON REBELLIOUS CHILDREN IN MINISTRY

Pastor's children come under special scrutiny and some do not fare well under the spotlight of criticism. A pastor and his wife have to recognize this danger and help their children to be able to handle the responsibility. It is important that the pastor's wife model before her children proper attitudes and not succumb to the natural reactions that promote resentment and eventually bitterness. In working with our staff wives, Carol always advised them to make the most of the time that they had with their husband rather than spending that time complaining.

I have seen the axiom be true in numerous situations that attitudes are caught not taught. It is only reasonable to expect that children will reflect the attitudes of their parents. If a pastor openly complains about people in the church or the spiritual leadership he has to work with, his wife and children will reflect these attitudes and may develop a resentment that impacts their spiritual growth. If a wife develops resentment for individuals or circumstances within the church it will eventually morph into a critical spirit and possible bitterness.

A critical spirit in ministry can often be diagnosed by answering the following questions:

1. Does the pastor chaff under the responsibility to be accountable to his elders or deacons?
2. Is the wife constantly complaining about the amount of time the husband is spending in ministry?
3. Does the father or mother take his children for granted, not considering their individual personalities and needs?

4. Is there no time for developing communication between members of the family?
5. Is the relationship between the parents one of constantly catching the children doing something wrong?
6. Is there no positive reinforcement when catching a child doing something right or noteworthy?
7. Do parents "fight" and put each other down in front of their children?
8. Is there consistency between what the church sees in a pastor and what his family experiences?
9. Is leadership in the home based upon authority or on influence?
10. Do the parents preach at the children or gently lead them in the discovery of truth?
11. Is violence tolerated as a way to solve differences?
12. Is respect for women modeled by the husband and expected of the sons?

Developing unity in the family takes investment on the part of parental leadership. One of the greatest deterrents to rebellion in a child is respect for his parents. That respect must be earned and not taken for granted. In our case we endeavored to build unity by emphasizing that when one achieved, we all shared in that achievement, and when one failed we all hurt together. There was no room for envy or jealousy. When it reared its ugly head, we lovingly confronted it with the teaching of God's Word. From the time our children were small we taught them that there were three things that were never tolerated in our home. Lying, direct disobedience and disrespect would be carefully confronted and consequences would follow. I am not saying that we were without mistakes in rearing our children. When we made mistakes, we acknowledged them and asked the children to forgive us.

ON FAMILY TIME

In the midst of a schedule that will certainly be demanding, the pastor must always appropriately set aside time for his family. My schedule was always very full, but I made appointments with my children to spend time with them. I always took each one out for his or her birthday to the restaurant of their choice. Their mother would help them get all dressed up and we treated it like a date with daddy. I tried to attend sporting events and take them Christmas shopping. Although it was sometimes very difficult, we tried to schedule a family night at least once a week.

On one such occasion we were scheduled to go Christmas shopping when I received a call from a young man whose wife had just had a baby. The child had been born with his heart outside his chest and he was in the Children's Hospital in Philadelphia. The young man's wife had been there constantly for several days and refused to leave and come home to get some rest. He wanted me to accompany him to the hospital to try to convince her to come home. I told him that I would get right back to him since I had an appointment that I had to change. I sat the children down and explained the situation to them and asked them what they thought I should do. Each one responded "Daddy, you have to go." My youngest replied, "Daddy, even selfish me says you have to go!" By approaching the decision in this way, I reinforced my children as part of my ministering team. It should be noted that we had a snowstorm overnight and school was canceled the next day. We were able to go to the mall and the Lord added an additional reward when the children found a $10 bill in the snow.

One of the most important times with our family was Sunday morning breakfast. Carol always baked blueberry muffins. I would go down to the church about 6:00 am to go over my sermon and spend time walking through the church praying for people as I passed their pew. When I completed my prayer time I would return home for breakfast with the family. They could see the road that led from the church from the breakfast nook and when the children saw me coming they would shout, "He's coming!" and everyone rushed to the table. When I came in to the breakfast table they would all sing "Good morning to you, good morning to you, we are all in our places with sunshiny faces and that is the way to start a good day." To this day our family repeats that same little song at our family gatherings.

ON PROTECTING THE PASTOR'S FAMILY

Guarding godly attitudes that encourage a love for the ministry is not easy. Invariably a pastor's children will be exposed to situations in ministry that are difficult. It is crucial that the responsible pastor help his children navigate such turbulent waters. One incident comes to mind when there was a particularly difficult church discipline process going on in our church. Because of the popularity of the individuals involved, our elders and I were the objects of great hostility. Our home was egged, our lawn marred by tire ruts and the most serious was a threat against my life. The latter came one afternoon when my fourteen year old daughter answered the phone only to have a lady scream at her that if we did not get out of town, they would kill me. Carol and I walked in the door finding her crying hysterically. We were faced with a test of helping our daughter respond properly to a very needy lady.

I took her in my arms to comfort her and to share with her that the woman who made the call had a great spiritual need that motivated her to make such a call. I urged her to join me on our knees to plead with the Lord on behalf of this woman. Praying for her had a wonderfully calming effect on my daughter and helped **us** to focus on the woman's need rather than on our fear. Years later our daughter was the roommate at college with the daughter of a politician from United Kingdom. The Queen had removed the man's bodyguard and his daughter's anger against the Queen burned hot. My daughter suggested that they go to their knees and pray for the Queen. Again, praying for your "enemy" had a calming effect, and my daughter again saw the fruit of lessons learned as "that preacher's kid."

Preparing a ministering team takes prayer and planning. It is not an easy road when recognizing that each child is unique. Developing family unity requires submission to the Holy Spirit's sanctifying leadership in ministry conduct. Attitudes must be constantly monitored in the lives of all involved. Spiritual growth must be the goal shared by all members of the family. When that goal is accomplished a ministering team is assured.

CHAPTER THREE

How Do I Provide Biblical Shepherding?

N ever ask someone to do something that you yourself are not willing to do.

Ken was our church custodian. Shortly after I became the pastor of Limerick Chapel, an incident occurred that solidified his confidence in me. Confidence is something that must be earned. Pastors and other spiritual leaders should not expect it to be automatically granted. The church owned a home used to house missionaries on furlough. A missionary family had occupied the home for several months and upon their departure the deacons ordered the carpets to be cleaned. It was a hot August and the home had been vacant for several weeks before arrangements could be made to clean the carpets. When the company arrived to do the job it found a stench in the house that prohibited the men from working. Ken and

I went to investigate and found that the missionary family upon their departure had followed an instruction sheet to the letter when it said to unplug all appliances. However, the freezer was full of meat placed there for the missionaries' use. Needless to say, when the freezer was unplugged, all this meat spoiled and had to be removed.

Certainly, I could expect that it was the janitor's job to do that, but I had always operated on the premise that I should not ask someone to do something that I was unwilling to do myself. So I said to Ken, "Let's get a garbage can, a couple of pails, and start to empty that freezer." He looked at me and said, "Are you going to help me?" I replied "Of course!" Together we took deep breaths, ran into the house, tried to fill our pails and then ran out before we had to breathe again. We repeated this until we had removed all the decaying meat. We then turned on the freezer to solidify all the "juice" still remaining. Ken was able to see me in a different light after the partnership we forged in the freezer incident.

ON THE BIBLICAL SHEPHERDING MODEL

There is so much Biblical information on pastoral ministry that it becomes necessary to sketch out a brief pastoral theology explaining the biblical model for the shepherd. I have often reflected upon the words of Paul when he shared with the Corinthian believers concerning the burden that came upon him daily. He called it *"the care of all the churches"* 2 Corinthians 11:28. His life was lived to please the Lord and to present the Lord's church to Him as a *"...chaste virgin..."* - 2 Corinthians 11:2. He knew the potential of the enemy to beguile and deceive the Lord's lambs and reminded the Corinthians that *"...we are not ignorant of his devices"* - 2 Corinthians 2:11. It is no wonder that Paul's prayer life was dominated by interceding in behalf of these young believers.

When Paul met with the Ephesian Elders in Acts 20:17-38, he rehearsed the way in which he had ministered among them. Several observations become evident from the text:

13. He served the Lord among them with humility.
14. He endured persecution by the Jews resulting in many tears and temptations.
15. He preached the whole counsel of God and kept back nothing that was profitable to them.
16. He taught both Jews and Gentiles publicly and privately from house to house declaring repentance toward God and faith toward the Lord Jesus.
17. He shared that an uncertain future in going to Jerusalem did not hinder him from his intention for ministry there.

18. He testified that his life was not dear to him, but his intention was to finish joyfully the ministry received of the Lord Jesus.

19. He states emphatically that he is free from the blood of all men for he has not shunned to declare unto them the whole counsel of God.

20.He notes that his ministry among them was voluntary and free from financial obligations on their part. He had supported himself and his coworkers through his trade. He was not chargeable to them.

He continues to admonish the Elders concerning their responsibilities with some pointed instruction: Acts 20:28

1. *"Take heed unto yourselves."* He is emphasizing the need to give careful attention to self examination concerning their spiritual preparedness for what lies ahead. v. 28

2. *"Take heed to the flock over which the Lord has made you overseers."* v. 28 Give careful attention to caring for the sheep.

3. *"Feed the church of God."* v. 28 Teach them by precept (the Word) and example.

4. Be prepared for the satanic *attacks* that will come both from without by grievous wolves and within by members of the body seeking to establish followers. v. 29

5. Remember the warnings I gave to you with tears while I was with you. v. 31

He calls attention to specific teachings concerning personal dedication to minister to people's needs:

1. Just as I taught you by my example, you should work hard to meet the needs of those who are both spiritually and physically void of strength. It can also refer to those who are sick. Acts 20:35 (cp. James 5:14)
2. Remember how I told you that the Lord taught that greater blessing comes from giving than from receiving. Acts 20:35
3. Before leaving them he knelt down and prayed with them. Acts 20:36

WHAT CAN WE LEARN ABOUT CARING FOR THE FLOCK FROM THE APOSTLE'S EXAMPLE?

First, he makes it plain that in his pastoral ministry he answers to the Lord first of all. The writer of Hebrews reiterates this principle in Hebrews 13:17 where he states *"... for they watch for your souls as they that must give an account...."* He served the Lord with humility of mind and with many tears along with many temptations. He was human and I am sure that he often was tempted to "move on." Three things in particular moved Paul to tears.

1. First, he grieved over the state of the lost. In Romans 9:2-3 he writes, *"I have great sorrow and unceasing grief in my heart. For I could wish that I myself were accursed, separated from Christ for the sake of my brethren, my kinsmen according to the flesh."*

2. Second, he cried over weak, struggling, sinning Christians. To such believers at Corinth he wrote, *"Out of much affliction and anguish of heart I wrote to you with many tears"* (2 Corinthians 2:4).

3. Finally, the sinister threat posed by false teachers caused Paul to say to the Ephesian elders, *"Therefore* [because of the false teachers mentioned in vv. 29-30] *be on the alert, remembering that night and day for a period of three years I did not cease to admonish each one with tears"* (v. 31). To the Philippians he wrote, *"For many walk, of whom I often told you, and now tell you even weeping, that they are enemies of the cross of Christ"* (Philippians 3:18).

Secondly, he regarded the church as the Lord's possession purchased with His own blood. He had no interest in self promotion nor did he exhibit a sense of ownership, but was willing to lay down his life on behalf of the people of God at Ephesus. He preached a dangerous message that brought the wrath of the Jews down upon him and he references their persistent persecution. In spite of the danger, he boldly preached without regard to his own safety. Some succumb to the temptation to "water down the message" and be politically correct and avoid addressing doctrines that are unpopular. I remember attending a seminar where the latest church growth approach was to avoid addressing subjects that would make people uncomfortable. I asked the question as to when it would be the appropriate time to allow people to know what we really believe. I was told, "That requires more study for when they finally realize what the church believes, it is possible that they will leave." It seemed like maintaining their presence was of primary importance and the church's programming and message reflected that priority. On another occasion my grandson called following a chapel at his Christian college. He shared how the chapel speaker had advised the student body to never tell people that they are sinners, in their witnessing techniques, for that may offend them. Following the chapel, my grandson approached the speaker to ask him how he could share the gospel without speaking about sin. The speaker responded that people know that they are sinners. My grandson's response was "You do not know the way my generation thinks, something is only a sin if you think it is a sin." Paul did not mince words; he held nothing back that was profitable for the health and growth of the Lord's flock. He shared the Word with great personal emotion and intensity knowing that God's people need meat if they are to survive in a godless society.

Thirdly, Paul knew the importance of being personally equipped in order to enter the battle to feed and protect the Lord's possession. When he wrote to the Ephesians a few years later, he reminded them of the nature of the enemy (Ephesians 6:11-12) and how to equip themselves for spiritual battles. This famous armor passage in Ephesians 6:10-18 details the way they could *withstand in the evil day having done all to stand."* It is important in our teaching ministry that the Word not only be taught in precept but that practical applications be shared. This demonstrates how to gain victory in the spiritual battle in which we find ourselves. Paul practiced this principle in writing Ephesians and Romans. The first three chapters of Ephesians and the first 11 chapters of Romans, he taught doctrinal precepts. The last three of Ephesians and the last five chapters of Romans Paul emphasized practical practice and responsibility. A good teacher both teaches and preaches the Word. Teaching helps the hearer to understand the doctrinal precepts, whereas preaching calls for personal action and helps the hearer to know how to use and apply the truth to issues in life. Philip Brooks described preaching as "Preaching is the communication of truth by man to men." (Brooks, Phillip, *Yale Lectures on Preaching*) This compliments the understanding of Richard Baxter when he says that "preaching is screwing the truth of God into the minds and hearts of men." (Baxter, Richard, *The Reformed Pastor*) The Psalmist said it most forcefully when he wrote *"Thy Word have I hid in my heart that I might not sin against thee"* Psalm 119:11.

One evening a young college student came to my home to admonish me. He said that I should avoid sharing applications of the Word to people's lives. He pointed out that a preacher should simply teach the precepts of the Word and let the Holy Spirit make the application. I shared with him the principle of the law of two witnesses. *"The Spirit bears witness with our spirit that we are children of God"* Romans 8:16. When declaring the truth, the Holy Spirit makes application but I feel responsible to lend my witness to human hearts concerning the validity of the Spirit's witness. He was disturbed by my personal applications to the character of true Christian living and later I found out that his alternate lifestyle was under spiritual attack by the Holy Spirit and he resented my calling attention to grossly unbiblical relationships and practices that were present in his life. Through the years I have found that opposing and exposing sexual sin from the pulpit makes those guilty uncomfortable and very critical. Paul reminds the Galatian Christians: *"Am I therefore become your enemy because I tell you the truth?"* Galatians 4:16.

Fourthly, Paul knew the importance of personal intimacy that flows from a caring leader. He points out that he had visited the Ephesian believers in their homes -Acts 20:20. His care for them was motivated by his love for the Lord and for the Lord's people. A leader that surrenders to the work of the Spirit of God that sheds abroad the love of God in his heart will gratefully have a love for the Lord's people. Someone has said that love is the spiritual fruit tree (Galatians 5:22) upon which all the rest of the fruit of the Spirit hang. Only the Spirit can produce a love for the unlovely and for our enemies. It should not be unusual that a godly leader have a special love for those in his care. People know when you genuinely love them. The principle is demonstrated in the precept *"We love God because He first loved us"* 1 John 4:19. John also indicates how we perceive the love of God when he wrote *"Hereby perceive we the love of God, because He laid down His life for us."* 1 John 3:16 He then follows this with the admonition *"Beloved, if God so loved us, we ought to love one another."* 1 John 4:11. Genuine love has no self interest.

I was standing near the Information Desk at Bob Jones University when a young man came up to me and asked, "You're Pastor Gregory aren't you?" I looked up at a tall young man and I had to confess, I didn't recognize him. I said you're going to have to help me with your name. He gave me his name and I immediately recognized who he was but I had not seen him in fifteen years. He related the following story to me: "I was six years old on your last Sunday at Limerick Chapel. I stood in line with my parents for what seemed to me to be an eternity in order to say good-bye. When our opportunity came, you knelt on the floor, looked me in the eye and said 'David, I want you to make me a promise. Will you promise me that you will serve the Lord and grow up to be a man of God?' Little did I know how that promise was to affect my life in years to come. There were many times when I was faced with decisions that my promise to my pastor came to my mind and helped me to avoid bad consequences. I have endeavored to keep that promise to you and to the Lord. I am graduating this year from BJU and I renew that promise that as for me and my house, we will serve the Lord."

You never know what a moment of personal intimacy with a child will bring. I always tried to know the children, call them by name and to kneel down, look them in the eye when speaking to them. It seals a relationship that will bring forth dividends as they grow into adults. Recently I received some cards from the sixth grade Sunday School Class at the Tabernacle Bible Church. They were precious and one in particular blessed my soul. The young man said that he never read the Bible before I came to be their pastor and he wanted to thank me for teaching him the importance of daily bible reading. Children are impressionable and a pastor should be careful to develop an intimacy with them that leaves lasting impressions.

ON LEADING BY EXAMPLE

It is of the utmost importance that a pastor practices this biblical model for shepherding in leading by example through modeling Christ likeness before the flock and its spiritual leadership. They need to be able to see his passion, his self control, his temperance, his selfless service, his love for all of the Lord's people, his servant's heart, his love for the Word, his humility and most of all the centrality of Christ in his life and ministry. This is a tall order but he must dedicate himself to servant leadership by example and precept in communicating his heart to the Lord's flock.

Leading by example is commanded of young Timothy in 1 Timothy 4:12 *"Let no man despise thy youth; but be thou an example of the believers, in word, in conversation, in charity, in spirit, in faith, in purity."*

Paul reminded the Philippians how Timothy had fulfilled that admonition when he wrote *Philippians 2:19 – 22:*

"But I trust in the Lord Jesus to send Timotheus shortly unto you, that I also may be of good comfort, when I know your state. For I have no man likeminded, who will naturally care for your state. For all seek their own, not the things which are Jesus Christ's. But ye know the proof of him, that, as a son with the father, he hath served with me in the gospel."

The Apostle made reference to his own leadership example in *2 Corinthians 11:24-28:* *"Of the Jews five times received I forty stripes save one. Thrice was I beaten with rods, once was I stoned, thrice I suffered shipwreck, a night and a day I have been in the deep; In journeyings often, in perils of waters, in perils of robbers, in perils by mine own countrymen, in perils by the heathen, in perils in the city, in perils in the wilderness, in perils in the sea, in perils among false brethren; In weariness and painfulness, in watchings often, in hunger and thirst, in fastings often, in cold and nakedness. Beside those things that are without, that which cometh upon me daily, the care of all the churches."* He reminds the Philippians, *"Those things which you have both learned, and received and heard, and seen in me, do..."*

Again, he challenges the Corinthians in *1 Corinthians 11:1:* *"Be followers (imitators) of me as I am a follower of Christ"* whose leadership example Peter cites in 1 Peter 2:21: *"...Christ also suffered for us, leaving us an example, that ye should follow in His steps..."*

ON HIDDEN AGENDAS

A spiritual leader must never have a "hidden agenda" he seeks to accomplish when he feels he has built his "power base" by the personal support of a significant number of people in the congregation. Transparency is important in defusing "suspicion" that some naturally have of leadership's motives.

When I came to Limerick Chapel as a potential candidate, I pointed out to the Deacon Board that if the church were to call me as pastor, I would have to attempt to bring the constitution and bylaws into agreement on the issue of membership. I noted that the Article IV on Doctrine had a very clear statement on the meaning and mode of baptism. In the section on membership in the by-laws it stated that potential members must agree with the doctrinal statement without reservation. However, later in the section it did not require baptism for membership. In essence, the documents stated that you must believe something that you were not required to practice. I shared that if I were to become pastor, I would seek to change this for I believed that I should never preach: "This is the truth, but you are not required to practice it." The church issued a call knowing my position and intention. I approached the revision carefully and patiently and it was not until eight years later that the change was made as a part of our entire document revision. I know of other situations where men have accepted a call, not agreeing with a doctrinal or procedural position, with the intention of changing the church when "I have established my base of support." When the hidden agenda is exposed, it results in a loss of confidence in the integrity of the leader.

This is certainly biblical. Paul cites the transparency of his leadership when he reminds Timothy in 2 Timothy 3:10-11: *"But Thou hast fully known my doctrine, manner of life, purpose, faith, longsuffering, charity, patience, persecutions, afflictions, which came unto me at Antioch, at Iconium, at Lystra; which persecutions I endured, but out of them all the Lord delivered me."*

ON BEING AMONG THE FLOCK

One of the ways a pastor can become "known" by both the church's spiritual leadership and its people is by heeding the advice of Peter in *1 Peter 5:1-3: "The elders which are among you, I exhort, who am also an elder, and a witness of the sufferings of Christ, and also a partaker of the glory that shall be revealed; Feed the flock of God which is among you, take the oversight thereof, not by constraint, but willingly, not for filthy lucre, but of a ready mind: Neither as being lords over God's heritage, but being ensamples of the flock."*

Notice how Peter emphasizes the fact of "among you." Spiritual leadership cannot isolate itself from those they seek to lead. They have to "get down and dirty" in the trenches and live and work among God's people. When I was a pastor in a rural community, I remember helping a farmer to put in the hay when rain was threatening and he needed an extra hand. One night my neighbor knocked on our door at 2:00 am to ask me if I could go with him to "rescue" his stalled truck. He needed me to steer it while he towed it home. I felt happy that he felt the freedom to ask his pastor for this kind of help.

Our approach was to have an open door policy at our home. We entertained gatherings of elders and deacons and their wives, Christmastime college and career events, youth social times and widows dinners. Sunday nights, after church we would host those who had been regularly visiting our church along with a deacon and elder and their wives. We were active in the fellowship groups and sought to always be available when needed, that included being available even during meals.

We did not take the telephone off the hook, and this policy led to several comical incidents when someone called while we were eating. Our children immediately began clanking their dishes prompting the question "Are you eating?" When I replied that our family was having dinner, I then would ask if I could call them back when we were finished with our devotional time.

People knew that if they had an emergency, they could always reach me. I once received a call during Christmas dinner telling me that one of the deacons had been taken to the hospital with a severe heart attack and the wife was not sure that he was alive. I dropped everything and rushed to the hospital to find that he had passed away. It was important that the wife be able to reach me because she needed her pastor to be there for her.

ON THE CONSEQUENCES OF ALOOFNESS

An aloof pastor will never be able to comprehend the frustrations and dreams of the people of the Lord's flock. People's responses and reactions are often colored by the circumstances being experienced in everyday life.

This was illustrated to me when I noticed a shift in one of the elder's attitudes. It became obvious that he was grasping after control in several areas. I had an opportunity to talk to his son who informed me that he was struggling because he had been moved aside in his very responsible job and was being marginalized in his leadership role. His company wanted him to retire and he was refusing to do so. It is hard to lose leadership influence and so he was attempting to replace it in his role as an elder. Understanding this helped me to come along side him and encourage him in his ministry as an elder. He was a valuable asset to the Lord's work and I tried to help him to see this even when he became a bit troublesome in meetings. Knowing what I knew enabled me to come to his defense.

I have known of circumstances where people felt that their pastor was unapproachable. I have had people come to me from other churches and when asked why they did not talk to their pastor, they replied, "He doesn't have time for the people in his congregation and he wouldn't understand anyway." It almost seems that some pastors conclude "The pastorate would be a marvelous ministry if it weren't for people!" Some pastors are CEOs and are dedicated to building their own kingdom where Christ and His people are not central but merely an aid in the accomplishment of their personal goals. This is contrary to the admonition to "be among the flock" and not "lording over the flock." The consequence of such aloofness is a lack of confidence in a man's shepherding ministry by those given to him to shepherd.

CHAPTER FOUR

How Do I Shepherd Difficult Sheep?

Pastoring in a small country church, the nearest hospital was fifty miles away. When someone in our flock was seriously sick, it was my responsibility to visit them. The distance to the hospital put a serious strain upon our budget, since we did not receive a car allowance. There was a local businessman in the church who employed a number of people in the congregation. He was a man a bit rough around the edges, but with a big heart and when he discovered the problem, he purposed to meet the need. He was used to making decisions on his own and proceeded to solve the problem on his own.

One day a backhoe arrived in the backyard of the parsonage and buried a gas tank which was promptly filled by a local fuel company. When the Board of Deacons inquired about who had authorized this, the company would not divulge the information. Later I found out that it was this businessman. It was his modus-operandi just to do something when he saw a need without asking permission.

One morning he came into my office and informed me that his wife was going to "take over" the responsibilities of the flower committee, and provide the flowers for the front of the church each Sunday because the present committee wasn't doing a job that met his approval. I shared with him that this was not appropriate. He then said that if I did not agree, that he would leave the church and we would not get one more red cent of his tithe. I pointed out that his tithe belonged to the Lord and that God did not want us to put strings upon our giving.

He promptly stormed out of the office and refused to come to church. I wanted to pursue him but decided to give the Lord time to do a work in him. His family remained in the church and consequently he would park his Cadillac at the curb each Sunday morning waiting to pick them up. When I opened the door following the service he would deliberately turn his head away. This took place for about six months. One day his son rushed to the parsonage and exclaimed: "Dad has just had a heart attack!" I jumped in my car, and was at his home before the ambulance. I knelt beside him as he lay on the floor, holding his hand and praying for him. He wouldn't let go of my hand and so I rode all of those fifty miles to the hospital with him. I knew that God had given me an opportunity to love and serve him in his hour of need. Even though he had proven to be a difficult sheep, it was still my responsibility to love him.

I later learned that reacting this way was a pattern that characterized him in previous pastoral relationships. However, his attitudes were markedly different following that brush with death. He became one of my close friends even after I moved from that ministry.

ON LOVING THE UNLOVELY

Learning to love unlovely believers who display their depravity can only be accomplished by the work of the Holy Spirit. Paul refers to the Fruit of the Spirit in Galatians 5:22 and notes that love is primary. There is always the evidence of the teaching ministry of the Holy Spirit in every true child of God. His teaching Carol and me how to love the unlovely was essential to a ministry among the spiritually immature. While not easy, the proper response to the promptings of the Holy Spirit led us in this transformation from natural resentment to love. One of the primary fruit of the Spirit in Galatians 5:22 is love.

One experience in particular prepared us for many traumas that we would face in the years to come. While

I was in seminary the Lord gave me the privilege of pastoring a small church. During one Christmas vacation, I visited this church to preach only to find out that the church had just gone through a split. I was anxious to preach, and when asked if I would return the next week to fill the pulpit, I readily accepted. The deacons soon asked if I would be interested in becoming their pastor. I agreed to have my name submitted to the congregation and the church extended a call.

Carol and I rejoiced in the opportunity. I was aware that although the split was over personalities, the remaining members were not the godliest. I soon found this to be true at a deacons meeting when two deacons almost came to blows over whether to have ice cream or watermelon at the Sunday School picnic. That incident was only a preview of things to come.

Our family soon experienced personal scrutiny like we never thought imaginable. Carol was "talked to" because she left our son's tricycle on the lawn overnight. They pointed out that the shades on the parsonage were not all pulled down at the same level. Sheets were still on the line one night a 9:00 PM because we had not arrived home from shopping and we were told that that was unacceptable. I was criticized because one Sunday my hair was too low on my forehead.

On and on the nitpicking went until I thought that we could take it no more. I called my dad and told him that while I was going to continue in seminary, I was going to resign the church and go sell cars at a local car dealer. His reply to me was rather disconcerting when he said, "That sounds like a good idea if you can get God's permission!"

I knew that running away was not the answer. As we talked together, my dear wife made this observation. "We have been asking God to change these people, maybe we are praying wrongly. Perhaps we should ask the Lord to change *our* hearts so that we can genuinely love them just the way they are." As soon as we made this commitment, the Lord faithfully began changing our attitude from self defense to heartfelt concern. He began to bless, and within three years, the twenty members at the beginning became one hundred and fifty. The original troublemakers were in the minority, and found themselves in trouble because new leadership arose and a different spirit began to characterize the church family.

Eventually it was exposed that the two "spiritual leaders" that were in charge when I arrived had serious spiritual problems. After I had left the church years later, I was told that one of them was keeping a woman and the other had questionable problems in his business and lost his insurance license. In spite of the problems we faced, the three years we spent in that church proved the best possible education. While not pleasant, we quickly learned that as a pastoral team, we had to be open to the work of the Holy Spirit enabling us to bear the Fruit of the Spirit "when the time for fruit bearing was right" - cp. Psalm 1.

As the above story illustrates, the ministry of the Holy Spirit is essential in the life of the spiritual leader. Understanding this role of the Spirit is vital to spiritual stability. It is of critical importance to also recognize that even the most difficult sheep still possess gifts of the Spirit. The maintenance of this perspective greatly assists the spiritual leader in his perspective on loving challenging individuals. If truly a part of the Body, then they are gifted for service in that Body.

There is great misunderstanding about the granting and administration of these spiritual gifts. When I was editor, we did a whole issue of the Voice Magazine (March-April 1996) that focused on the work of the Holy Spirit in a believer's life. It emphasized the fruit that the Holy Spirit produces in and through the believer. When the believer reflects the character of the Lord Jesus, it is the Holy Spirit that must receive the credit. It is His task to conform every child to the image of Christ (Romans 8:28-29) for it is the destiny of every believer ultimately to be like the Lord Jesus. John speaks of this in 1 John 3:1-2 when he writes:

"Behold what manner of love the Father has bestowed upon us that we should be called the sons of God; therefore, the world

knows us not, because it knew Him not. Beloved, now are we the sons of God, and it does not yet appear what we shall be, but we know that when He shall appear we shall be like Him."

The Holy Spirit will do His job in every true believer through gentle leading or through the trauma of disciplinary teaching. Hebrews 12:11 speaks to this when it says: "Now no chastening for the present seemeth to be joyous, but grievous: nevertheless afterward it yields the peaceable fruit of righteousness unto them who are exercised by it." Understanding the Spirit's role in gifting and disciplining His people provides great freedom to the shepherd. When you understand the Spirit moves in the hearts of difficult sheep, you are free to love and shepherd them after the sovereign leading of God's Spirit.

ON PEACEMAKING

Human beings have an innate ability to be selfish. It arises from their fallen nature. Again it is only the presence of the Holy Spirit enabling believers to seek the unity that overcomes the petty differences that are the source of so many conflicts within the church. Throughout the epistles, Paul cites a number of circumstances where conflict existed within the church of Corinth. Their unity was fractured by believers following after individuals. Some said: "I am of Paul," while others identified with Apollos, Cephas or even

Christ. Paul calls these contentions contrary to the unity that is in Christ - 1 Corinthians 1:11-13 & 3:4-6.

Other scriptural illustrations of potential problems within the life of the church are:

At the church of Philippi: Paul actually names two women that are at odds in Philippians 4:2. In that passage, he calls upon Euodias and Syntyche to seek the unity of being of the same mind in the Lord.

At the church of Rome: Paul warned the Roman believers to identify those who cause divisions and offenses contrary to sound doctrine and avoid them - Romans 16:17.

At the church of Colossae: Paul warned the Colossian believers to *"Beware lest any man spoil you through philosophy and vain deceit after the tradition of men after the rudiments of the world, and not after Christ"* - Colossians 1:8. He further instructed them that some would rob them of their reward by emphasizing *"voluntary humility and worshipping of angels, intruding into those things which he has not seen, vainly puffed up by his fleshly mind, and not holding the Head from which all the body by joints and bands having nourishment ministered and knit together, increases with the increase of God"* - Colossians 2:18-19.

How do servant leaders respond when conflict raises its ugly head within the church that the Lord has called them to shepherd? There are several approaches that leaders often take:

1. **The Ostrich Approach:** *Ignore the problem hoping that it will go away.* This approach is often taken by those who hate confrontation and will go to great lengths avoid it. While I understand that actions do affect the body and consequences need to be carefully evaluated, the result of this approach will always produce a quenching of the Spirit of God and will ultimately adversely affect the church's ability to be salt and light in its community.

   A pastor once approached me sharing that one of his church planting missionaries had fallen into moral sin. He said that some of the deacons at the church plant were prone to have the missionary resign and quietly go away. These deacons had concluded that to make his sin public would cause problems in the church. I asked him what did he think would happen when the church found out that leadership had covered this up? I also asked him if the leadership's approach was best for the fallen brother? The pastor already knew that the "Ostrich Approach" did not fulfill the instruction given in 1 Timothy 5:19-20: *"Against an elder receive not an accusation, but before two or three witnesses. Them that sin, rebuke before all, that others may fear."* We had a time of sharing how to best minister to those deacons in that fledgling church and the roll his church would play in the discipline process.

2. **The Iron Fist Approach:** *The use of your raw leadership authority.* This approach confronts and demands that the parties involved repent and be reconciled. Leading by exercising authority always produces resistance. This resistance can manifest itself in an attempt to deflect responsibility based upon what someone else did or said. The very nature of confession is agreeing with what God's Word says about an attitude or action. Sin must be recognized as sin; but, just calling it sin does not produce repentance. When repentance is demanded the sinner often will provide insincere repentance to avoid consequences or to cover his shame.

I remember a circumstance when a young couple shared that when they became expectant parents outside of marriage that the pastor demanded that they go before the church and confess their sin. They fulfilled the requirement but a number of years later they shared with me that the only reason they complied was to have a church wedding and to get the church off their backs. Needless to say, there was no genuine fruit of repentance and their Christian lives were plagued by unresolved sin against the Lord and each other. One pastor described unfruitful repentance as shame management

- willing to draw upon the Christian virtue of forgiveness on the part of God's people without ever genuinely repenting of sin.

3. **The Biblical Approach:** *Become a peacemaker.* This approach recognizes that God's love is showered equally upon those believers on all sides of a conflict. It is important to be convinced of this great truth. None of God's children are our enemies. They are brothers and as Paul instructs the Thessalonian believers to *"Count not a disagreeing brother as an enemy, but admonish him as a brother"* - 2 Thessalonians 3:15. Paul reminds the Galatian believers: *"Am I become your enemy because I tell you the truth?"* - Galatians 4:17. When Paul cited the two women in Philippians and encouraged them to be of the same mind in the Lord, he asked "True Yokefellow" as well as Clement and the other believers to help them in their reconciliation - Philippians 4:2-3.

True repentance and reconciliation requires personal ministry on the part of a believer, or believers. One must become involved in seeking the unity necessary to overcome unbiblical attitudes that always characterize conflict. Remember, God is never in a hurry. He gives us time to change and uses His servants who come alongside to help that change happen.

Being a peacemaker means to treat all sides of a conflict with the same concern and model true humility in seeking the *"...unity of the Spirit in the bond of peace"* Ephesians 4:3. One Russian brother noted: "When godly men have the same God, the same Holy Spirit, the same Word of God and the same love for each other, there is no conflict that cannot be resolved in a godly manner."

One Sunday morning I noticed one of the ladies in the congregation sitting with folded arms and with her back turned away from her husband. Her body language indicated that something was drastically wrong. When they came out the door where Carol and I were greeting the people, I did something that I had never done before or since. As she tried to slide past me, I reached out and putting my hands on her shoulders turned her toward me and asked "When are you going to deal with your bitterness and anger?"

She exclaimed "Well!" and stormed out with her husband following her in tears. Carol turned to me and said "Honey, why in the world did you do that?" I sheepishly replied "I don't know!" Tuesday, I received a call from this lady and as I took the call I expected to hear sharp criticism. Instead, the lady asked "Pastor why did you do that?" I gave her the same answer I gave to my wife "I don't know." The lady then replied "Maybe the Lord does love me. I was planning to send my family off to church and while they were away I was planning on committing suicide. I didn't want to live anymore." My wife and I spent many hours with this couple over the next months. We found out that she had great bitterness toward her mother and had kept her children from getting to know her though she lived about 20 miles away. We laid out some steps where she could initiate reconciliation beginning by sending a letter to her. It was very hard to do this but the day she finally sent it we all went out to dinner to celebrate. Eventually full reconciliation did take place and when the mother became sick with cancer, this once very bitter daughter took her into her home and cared for her until her death.

ON PRIDE AS A SOURCE OF CONFLICT

Early in my ministry I experienced bold-faced pride on the part of a member of the church. We were having evangelistic meetings and when the invitation was given a young teacher came forward to be saved. Her father, one of the deacons, jumped up and exclaimed, "She's saved! She is the only person that I have ever led to the Lord and you are not going to take that away from me." The evangelist and I were shocked. Being young, I did not know how to handle the situation.

Years later, there was an incident with a different person in a testimony meeting where a man began to castigate the congregation for its lack of care for him. This time I quietly came down from the pulpit and put my arm around him. I assured him that I cared for him and would give him some personal time to talk about his concerns but reminded him quietly that this was not the proper forum for these comments.

This same individual approached me after the service one Sunday night and informed me that he thought that I was very arrogant because I spoke so definitely about things and he wanted me to know that he knew more about the Word than I did. I told him that I appreciated the fact that he felt he could be honest with me and that I would carefully examine my attitudes. It took him back that I did not react to his accusations but received them in a positive way. I asked him to pray for me that I might be humble and learn from his criticism. It was the first step in establishing a relationship with him and when I retired from that ministry I received a card from him that said that he considered me to be one of the best teachers he ever knew. A humble response to overt pride opened up the door to being able to minister to him.

Pride manifests itself in many ways and sometimes it takes an observer to point it out in a person. Leadership needs to recognize that personal criticism is often grounded in something that a person feels justified in pointing out. It may not be the real reason why a person is being critical. Leadership needs to respond to criticism and search for the kernel of truth in the criticism rather than reacting by dismissing it based upon its source.

ON POWER STRUGGLES AS A SOURCE OF CONFLICT

It is often hard for men who are successful in their endeavors, whether it be business or labor management, to make the transition from being a lone decision maker to being a part of a team where consensus is important and unity is the goal. I remember an individual that was very successful on Wall Street coming to me and informing me that I was not to preach on money since he took care of the finances in the little church where I was the pastor. He said that he would make the decisions on what kind of money the church needed and he would supply the funds needed. I was faced with a power struggle that could have split the church. I asked for some personal time with him and went over my message on giving, sharing with him my view that giving was part of our worship and all should give what they can. I shared that I would not be preaching the whole counsel of God if I neglected teaching on giving. He reluctantly agreed that I should teach but not make people feel guilty if they could not give. Unity, not total agreement was achieved.

Power struggles within the Body are a part of the nature of our depravity. We like things to go our way and when they don't the natural tendency is to seek out those who agree and try to line up support. This tendency can manifest itself among the people of the congregation as well as among the spiritual leadership. Dividing the body in this way is always non productive in the quest for unity. Building a sense of inter-dependence with good teaching on seeking the mind of the Lord will help believers to resist their depravity and submit to the clear leading of the Spirit in such situations. It is important that spiritual leadership model this humility by not insisting that they always get their way.

ON STRONG ARM TACTICS AS A SOURCE OF CONFLICT

"I'll show them who is boss." This can be the by line of those that try to *"lord over the flock."* Peter is very specific about the unbiblical nature of this approach. He instructed the elders in 1 Peter 5:2-3: *"Feed the flock of God which is among you, taking the oversight thereof, not by constraint, but of a ready mind; neither as being lords over God's heritage, but being examples to the flock."* Appealing to one's position and authority does not reflect the leadership style of the Lord Jesus. In fact leading by using your influence will result in followers while leading by using your position or authority will always produce resistance and suspicion. People will tend to react with "Who does he think he is? Just because he is the pastor doesn't mean...." Influence is summed up in *"being examples to the flock."* Authority is summed up in *"being lords over God's heritage."*

ON RUMORS, LIES AND GOSSIP AS A SOURCE OF CONFLICT

The Lord described Satan as a *"... liar from the beginning and the father of lies"* - John 8:44. Although no believer is our enemy, believers can be used by Satan. He often seduces them into using his methods, one of which is to spread destructive rumors and half truths. He seduced Ananias and Sapphira to lie to the Holy Spirit about their claims concerning their giving. Paul warns Titus that *"...Cretans are always liars..."* and noted that Titus should *"...rebuke them sharply that they may be sound in the faith"* - Titus 1:12.

Proverbs, in the section on a father instructing his son, includes a "lying tongue" as one of the six things that God hates - Proverbs 6:17. John lists liars among the most heinous sins in Revelation: *"But the fearful and unbelievers, and the abominable, and murders, and whoremongers, and sorcerers, and idolaters, and all liars, shall have their part in the Lake that burns with fire and brimstone: which is the second death."* - Revelation 21:8.

James points out that sins of the heart are manifested by an uncontrolled tongue. This is the source
of great conflict. Jesus said *"... out of the abundance of the
heart the mouth speaks"* - Luke 6:45, and James points out
that *"...the tongue is a world of iniquity and boasts great things.
... It is an unruly evil, full of deadly poison."* - James 2:6–8.
The words spoken by the tongue can be a blessing
or a curse. Believers should pray every day that the
Lord would *"set a watch, O Lord, before my mouth; keep the
door of my lips, incline not my heart to any evil thing, to practice
wicked works with men that work iniquity..."* - Psalm 141:3-4.
Proverbs condemns tale bearing and chronicles the
result. *"The words of a talebearer are as wounds, and they go
down into the innermost parts of the belly"* - Proverbs 18:8;
and makes this observation: *"...where there is no talebearer,
the strife ceases"* - Proverbs 26:20.

I remember an incident when a man in our church
came to me and shared that he had been working in
the basement of one of our elders and had observe
that there was a case of beer there. He was really
exercised about this and wanted me to do something
about this apparent contradiction in standards by one
of our spiritual leaders. I asked him if he had spoken to
the elder about his observation. As I expected, he had
not. I urged him to seek an explanation directly from
the elder. Later he came to me and reported that in
talking with the elder, he found out that his unsaved

father-in-law was visiting and the case belonged to him. If the observation had been shared with others it could have been very damaging to an elder's ministry.

It is important that believers understand that our fallen natures tend to rejoice in iniquity when we hear a juicy bit of gossip about another believer. My son called me from college one day to share with me some information about a spiritual leader that seemed to confirm what people were expecting to happen. Before I allowed him to share what he had heard, I asked him several questions. "Why do you think I need to know this? How do you feel sharing this information will help you spiritually? Does it make you sad that a spiritual leader has compromised in this matter? Has receiving this information caused you to pray for this man? If you still feel that I should know what you have heard, call me tomorrow and we will discuss this." Needless to say, he did not approach the subject again and he later told me that asking himself these questions helped to protect him from *"rejoicing in iniquity"* - 1 Corinthians 13:6.

ON DEALING WITH STUBBORNNESS

There are some people that will always vote "no" on every issue. Once a man told me that he always voted no as a matter of principle because he believed that nothing should ever be unanimous. I once belonged to a congregation where you could predict the number of "no" votes. My estimate was always within one or two votes on every issue. These were people that did not want the pastor and the elders to have "too much power" and they felt that opposing those things being suggested was a way in which they could accomplish this. Unless the "peacemaker" can establish a working relationship with situations like this, conflicts are always inevitable. The pastor was very gracious in these situations and allowed time and discussion to take place on every issue. When critical or unkind comments were made in a business meeting, he did not put that person down but offered them time to meet with the elders to have their case considered. His patient graciousness eventually dispelled the suspicious attitudes of the "no crowd" and some semblance of unity began to grow.

ON THE ESSENTIAL INGREDIENT FOR UNITY

Paul in Ephesians shares with the Believers in Ephesus:, *"I therefore the prisoner of the Lord, beseech you that you walk worthy of the vocation wherewith you are called, with all lowliness and meekness, with longsuffering, forbearing one another in love; endeavoring to keep the unity of the Spirit in the body of peace"* - Ephesians 4:1-3. I believe that this verse identifies the essential qualities in biblical humility. When one *"humbles himself under the mighty hand of God"* - 1 Peter 5:6, he surrenders both his preferences and the results of submitting problems to the Lord for solutions. He does not demand his way but is willing to learn to disagree agreeably and seek the common ground of oneness in the Lord. This is done by recognizing that those who disagree are not enemies but brothers. When two parties both have their eyes fixed upon the Lord they will have a oneness described by John: *"That which we have seen and heard, declare we unto you, that you also may have fellowship with us, and truly our fellowship is with the Father and with His Son Jesus Christ"* - 1 John 1:3.

True biblical unity does not demand agreement. It requires the qualities of humility that are characterized by lowliness, long suffering, forbearance and unity. This unity walks hand in hand with biblical love which *"... seeks not her own and is not easily provoked"* - 1 Corinthians 13:5, resulting in *"... being of the same mind in the Lord"* - Philippians 4:2.

Paul's ministry was more than teaching the precepts of God's Word. His personal practice modeled love and concern for God's people and he left those within the church having a deep and abiding love for him. It should be the goal of all spiritual leaders that they finish well and that God's people are sad to see them go.

I come from a large family with three older sisters and five younger brothers. Though my father only went to the fourth grade because of the death of his father, we all recognized his unusual ability to be well informed on almost any subject that came up for discussion. He worked at a local newspaper as a linotype operator and had almost perfect recall of the facts he set into type, even to the racing charts. My mother was a teacher and education was a priority in our family. The question was not "do you want to go to college?" but "where?" Consequently, the family became very diverse. There were undergraduates of Bob Jones University, Robert Packer Hospital Nursing School, Shelton College, Moody Bible Institute, Wheaton College, Biola and Cedarville University. In addition several held graduate degrees from Faith Seminary, Gordon Seminary and Harvard. This provided a diversity and fodder for lively discussion. However, there were strong family ties and when anyone had a problem we all shared. We had family unity and mutual respect, even though we were divided philosophically, politically and in some matters of faith. Being in agreement was not often present but we all cherished the fact that we were "Gregorys." Even today the strong family identity is evident when every three years we have a family reunion and people travel from all over the United

States to spend time together. Hugs and expressions of joy at seeing one another makes the reunion an awesome occasion.

The church is also a "family." It is diverse with people coming from all kinds of backgrounds and experiences. Although there is room for a variety of opinions on various subjects, we find our identity in Jesus Christ. This mystical identity manifests itself in a love for the church and its people. There is no room in a church family for jealousy, grudges, evil speaking or a variety of other strained interpersonal relationships. Our disagreements must never be characterized by refusing to speak to a brother or sister, destructive gossiping, harboring of bitterness, malice or unforgiveness. Through the years I have encountered such things in fractured family relationships and even among confessing Christians. This ought not to be so and when it occurs, spiritual leadership has the responsibility to confront the individuals involved and lead in the quest for reconciliation. Matthew 18:15-17 provides the solution for fractured interpersonal relationships. Failure to accomplish reconciliation has drastic consequences for those unwilling to respond. Church discipline is the Lord's answer to the display of anger and bitterness in rebelling against the unity that is a character quality of born again believers in their relationships.

CHAPTER FIVE

How Do I Work with My Staff?

ON THE NATURE OF STAFF

A pastor's ministry staff must be an extension of his ministry. There are several important characteristics that must be present in order that this be true. Staff members should have the same philosophy of ministry as the pastor. If one does not it will eventually bring him or her into conflict with the pastor. I experienced this when a youth pastor ignored specific instructions to reach out to the parents of the youth that were attending public school. The church had a thriving Christian Academy and most of our youth were students there. I perceived that the families that had chosen public education for their children felt like they were being ignored. After several meetings with the youth pastor he finally admitted his reluctance to develop a dimension of ministry especially designed to reach out to public school kids. He felt his time could be used most effectively by placing his attention of those whose parents were seeking a Christian education for their children. Needless to say, I did not agree with him for I felt that the young people facing the secular influences every day needed special attention. These parents could use the encouragement of the church's ministry to them by helping equip them to shepherd their children through these influences. All I wanted from him was a plan to reach out to the parents and students in public school. When he continued to ignore my wishes I gave him a choice. He could be immediately dismissed for insubordination or he could have ninety days to find another ministry. If he chose the ninety days we would give him a "going away send off," but if I heard one word about our conversation, he would be dismissed immediately. He decided to go back to school and a number of years later he confided in me that what had taken place was the best thing that could have happened to him. He later had a successful ministry as a youth pastor.

ON LOYALTY AMONGST STAFF

Additionally, staff members should have a fierce loyalty to the pastor. This loyalty demands that they be willing to share their hearts and understandings of the ministry in personal sessions with him. If they see something where they feel the pastor is failing or is weak, staff members should be free to offer to assist the pastor in shoring up his ministry. The pastor will foster the confidence in his staff to do this by being willing to be a good listener and recognizing that in the multitude of counselors there is wisdom. It will also give the pastor the opportunity to share the reasons behind an action or position. A silent staff member will eventually become a resentful staff member whose unvoiced dissatisfactions morph into a critical spirit.

Just as it is expected that a pastor's staff be loyal to his leadership so a pastor should be a loyal shepherd to those serving under that leadership. One of the ways that will assist in this relationship is the "chain of command" in the church's organizational chart. It is very difficult for a staff member when he answers to more than one leader. Recognizing that ultimately a staff member is responsible to the governing board, the pastor should be the one to whom the staff member answers in his day to day ministry. I asked board members to "go through me" if there were any questions concerning a staff members ministry. It worked well and the staff appreciated the clarity of supervising relationships. If I were to see something among the teachers in the Academy that I questioned, I would talk to the Principal rather than approach the teacher myself. If the Principal wanted to include me in the matter, it would be his decision. It is important that you allow staff members to handle problems within their sphere of ministry. It gives them confidence that you trust them.

ON HONESTY WITH STAFF

A Senior Pastor needs to be open and honest with individual staff members. When a new staff member came in for a personal session with me he shared that he was really frustrated. He had just graduated from seminary and had joined our staff. He shared that he felt that the congregation didn't respect his seminary degree. I sat there for a moment and then replied, "This does not surprise me for neither do I." I pointed out to him that respect is something that you earn. One should not expect that it be granted just because you have a degree. I noted that his degree meant much to him because he had worked hard to achieve it, but people are more concerned about attitudes, demonstrated love for them and servant leadership. We talked about how he could gain their love and respect through personal involvement in people's lives and demonstrating a real servant's heart. It was important that this feeling of frustration be dealt with as a possible cause of discouragement and an indication that change of perspective was needed. He made the transition and for several years had a productive ministry before moving on to a Senior Pastorate of his own.

ON MINISTRY DESCRIPTIONS

Ministry Descriptions are essential to staff effectiveness. Staff members need to know what they are responsible for and to whom they should look for leadership. It has always been my leadership style to share the end that I envisioned in a ministry and then ask the staff member to share how he thinks we can accomplish this. A ministry description should not just describe responsibilities, but should include the requirement of visioning and sharing how ministries can be most effective. If there is no creativity in a staff member, he is unworthy of his ministry. It is not enough to say "Tell me what to do and I will do it." My method was to say "This is what I want to accomplish, now tell me how we can realize our goals"

One of the staff responsibilities was to be the liaison between the Elder Committee assigned to them and the Pastor. Church oversight was divided between six committees each chaired by an Elder with a pastoral staff member assigned to each committee. These staff members attended the committee meetings along with other members of the committee from the congregation at large. This provided a bridge between the committees and the pastoral staff.

ON STAFF MEETINGS

Our weekly staff prayer meetings gave each of us an opportunity to gaze into the hearts of those with whom we work. We did not verbally share prayer requests before we went to prayer, but each staff member prayed about those things on his heart. The regular weekly staff meetings were not as sedate but were often characterized by lively discussions on administrative procedures, substance and the latest trends in theology, music and church growth. Sometimes it was necessary for me to overrule an action taken by a staff member but I tried to do so in private. On one such occasion the Superintendent and Principal of our Academy reported that men from the local fire company had just walked into the school unannounced and pulled the fire alarm. They were confronted by the administration and asked to leave. A crusading "Christian" lawyer had stated in a seminar that you do not have to let them come on your property. I was deeply disturbed by this incident and immediately called the fire chief and asked to have a few minutes in their weekly meeting. We went to the meeting and the men apologized to the firemen for their impulsive response. I assured the firemen that we would cooperate with them in the future but asked them if they would be willing to check with our school calendar so that their unannounced fire drills did not conflict with our upcoming placement testing program. They readily agreed. I then issued an invitation to the fire company to tour our building with its maze of stairs, hallways and rooms so that if we did have a fire the firemen would be familiar with our building layout. We hosted the tour with coffee and donuts. This initiative on our part went a long way to maintaining a good relationship with one of our community organizations.

ON UNITY WITH STAFF

The seventeen years I spent as pastor of Limerick Chapel was characterized with few exceptions by a harmonious staff atmosphere. Consequently we enjoyed staff longevity. The six men on our staff served with me an accumulative total of over sixty years. Staff stability was a blessing both I and the church thoroughly enjoyed. However, after I left Limerick, I inherited a staff where I had to establish my leadership all over again. This proved to be difficult and several situations developed while I was traveling that heightened tension. Disagreement on leadership style and production expectations finally came to a head and two staff members had to be let go. Once they were out of the office, I was free to administrate without undermining influences. Sometimes it is difficult to solve staff problems without drastic action. It is important that the governing board be included in your concerns and that you listen to their insights concerning endeavors to solve the conflicts. It was not my desire to let these staff members go and on several occasions I requested of the governing board more time to solve the problems. After numerous efforts on my part the governing board finally acted and terminated their service. Inheriting a staff often has dangerous pitfalls associated with it especially if some regard you as an "outsider." In my case I endured several years of destructive murmuring that eroded my leadership ability. Once that was removed, the remaining staff proved to possess the loyalty and support a leader needs to effectively lead a ministry and my remaining time with the organization, I enjoyed the same harmonious atmosphere I was used to at the Chapel.

ON PERSONAL RELATIONSHIPS AMONG THE STAFF

A close personal relationship demonstrated between staff members goes a long way in building strong cooperative ministry. Staff outings, retreats and social gatherings are important in bringing the staff families together. A church staff is the source of a ministry's effectiveness in meeting the goals agreed upon by the church's spiritual leadership. It is therefore incumbent upon a pastor to build a strong staff and to seek to maintain its unity.

ON CHOOSING STAFF

Choosing the right person to fill a ministry leadership position is very important. It is a fallacy to think that you can call a person and then create a ministry for him. When that takes place leadership often falls into the pitfall of "pounding square pegs into round holes." Ministry descriptions should be carefully constructed and then a person should be sought who is gifted in the dimensions that ministry demands. The church staff can be a blessing or an albatross around a pastor's neck. Choosing correctly and then carefully "pastoring" the members of a pastoral staff is primary in accomplishing a work for the Lord.

ON DEVELOPING FUTURE PASTORS AND MISSIONARIES

One of the dimensions of a church staff is to be involved in developing those that believe they have been called to ministry. I have always had a burden for those that are aspiring to "full time service." While at Laceyville, I mentored a young man who was studying at a local Bible College. When I came to Limerick, I was able to establish an intern program that eventually included a dozen of our own young people who were in college preparing for ministry . They were taken under care by our Elders and spent the summers working with our staff in various ministries, one of which was to supervise our teens in conducting summer neighborhood bible clubs. It_was a three year program. Each year they were given additional responsibilities. We provided a scholarship for their college costs. I wanted to sand off their rough edges rather than subject them to the drama of having them knocked off by others in their first church.

ON SMALL CHURCHES

Much of what I have written is in the context of a large church with several staff members. Having pastored two small churches where I was the only paid staff, I recognize how important small churches are in the advancement of the kingdom. I am aware that often the pastor in a small church is asked to wear several hats. But even in small churches there are men serving as elders or deacons that can be trained to assume shepherding ministries. One of the primary tasks of a pastor of a small church is to train leaders who will assume oversight of the flock in the absence of a pastor. Just as we tell missionaries it is their responsibility to work themselves out of a job by training successors from among nationals, so it is the pastor's responsibility to assure the churches fidelity to the word of God and sound theology by training men in these disciplines.

My son pastors a church of about 300. Each Saturday morning he conducts a class teaching his men systematic theology. In the past several years of this practice numerous men have completed the four-year course. Training men to recognize false doctrine and aberrant philosophies of ministry is **an** inherent part of developing leadership.

The principles set forth in this book can be applied to a large multi-member staff or to that of a pastor of a small church and its spiritual leadership. The key is seeking the unity of purpose and philosophy in the application of these principles.

CHAPTER SIX

How Do I Slay the Dragons in Ministry?

ON THE NATURE OF SPIRITUAL WARFARE

How do we neutralize and defeat the schemes of the devil as he seeks to corrupt the spiritual walk of God's children? The Apostle Peter warned believers in 1 Peter 5:8 to *"be sober, be vigilant: because your adversary the devil, as a roaring lion, walks about seeking whom he may devour."* Paul shared with the Corinthians in 2 Corinthians 2:11 that they should be careful to maintain a forgiving spirit *"Lest Satan should get an advantage of us: for we are not ignorant of his devices."* It is important that believers take seriously the warnings of these two spiritual giants. It should be noted, however, that when believers concentrate on the enemy rather than on the One who has defeated the enemy, that is on Christ, they are playing right into Satan's strategy. Someone has said that the way to defeat the efforts of Satan in one's life is to remember that *greater is He that is in you, than he that is in the world"* - 1 John 4:4. Successfully resisting the devil is accomplished by turning to the Person and work of Jesus Christ on the cross. Through His defeat of death by His resurrection He is demonstrated to be the powerful Son of God – cp. Romans 1:4. If one decides that he is able to defeat the devil by following the formulas of those involved in so called "spiritual warfare" then one is destined to disillusionment and frustration. It may result in temporary victories that are used by the enemy to promote pride and self confidence. Just when you thought that you had the devil on the run, he turns on you with renewed subtlety and deception.

Scripture does, however, suggest that the mere presence of believers inhibits Satan's power and program. Paul, in his discussion of the events surrounding the Lord's return, reminds the Thessalonian believers that *"...he who now hinders will continue to hinder until he be taken out of the way"* - 2 Thessalonians 2:7. I understand this to be a reference to the Holy Spirit who dwells within the church through believers. The presence of these believers inhibits Satan from implementing his plan and only after the church is raptured will the anti-Christ be revealed. I recently heard the great grandson of a Voodoo witch doctor in Haiti, testify that when his grandmother trusted Christ, her father's Voodoo powers would not work when she was in the house. Consequently she was asked to leave.

On The Danger of Demon Possession There was a family in the church where I was the pastor that befriended and reached out to their daughter's roommate at a Christian college in New England. She came from a family where her mother was involved in witchcraft. She claimed to be saved and so this family, wanting to encourage her, invited her to stay with them in their home over the summer. One evening I received a frantic call from the family sharing that this young lady was sitting in their living room making guttural sounds and foaming at the mouth. They asked me to come quickly. When I arrived and walked into the room, she jumped up and charged across the room at me. I was surprised by this and threw up my arms to protect myself. I was holding my Bible in my hands. When she was about two feet from me it appeared as if she hit a wall. She fell backwards and crumpled onto the floor.

I had no experience in "casting out demons" and really didn't know what to do. So with Bible in my hand I knelt and commanded the demons to depart from her. Suddenly, my Bible flew out of my hands and I made a dive to retrieve it. I then said "through the power of the finished work of Christ on the cross and His shed blood, I command you to come out of her." She gave a scream and fainted. Several minutes later she revived and seemed to be perfectly normal. She said that she had no recollection of the incident. Several days later I received another call. When I arrived I was taken to her bedroom where she was lying on the floor with her head in the closet. No one announced my arrival but she said in a guttural voice: "he's here, I want him to see this." I had done some research on situations like this so again appealing to the power of the finished work of Christ I commanded the demons to identify themselves. In the same guttural voice I heard such names as "the love of women, lying, deception and other sins." When I commanded them to be bound and come out of her she jumped up ran past us and collided full force into the wall at the end of the hall. She fell down screaming, writhing on the floor and then passed out.

Several minutes later she revived and appeared to be perfectly normal. In my counseling sessions with her she shared how that on one Sunday evening she used her "powers" to put people to sleep while I was preaching. I had my doubts about this for on that particular Sunday night I was preaching from Isaiah's vision of God in Isaiah 6 and a number of people responded to the invitation. She soon returned to New England and we never heard from her again. Was she a messenger from Satan to lure us into the belief that we had power over Satan only to have him demonstrate that he was still in control of this young lady? Was her presence designed to challenge my belief that a true believer cannot be possessed by demons? She was attending a Christian College and testified to personal salvation. Before these incidents, I had baptized her and she was scheduled to meet with the Elders about church membership. It made me aware that all professing Christians are not genuine born again believers.

I have talked to several other pastors that had similar experiences and they related to me that ultimately their efforts proved insufficient and discouraging. I, like the others, am hesitant to talk about this very traumatic time in my life. It made me aware that Satan has his "agents" scattered among believers to accomplish His ends. *"And no marvel, for Satan himself is transformed into an angel of light. Therefore it is no great thing if his ministers also be transformed as the minister of righteousness whose end shall be according to their works"* - 2 Corinthians 11: 14-15

The great danger in "taking on the devil" is the false impression that one has the power to bind his demons and release someone from his power. Even *"Michael, the archangel, when contending with the devil, he disputed about the body of Moses, dared not to bring against him a railing accusation, but said, the Lord rebuke you"* - Jude 9. Since the devil is so powerful, can people be released from his power? Certainly, but only if that individual turns to Christ to break the chains that bind him. Resisting the devil is certainly biblical (1 Peter 5: 9) but it is accomplished by living consistently for Christ and focusing on Him. The answer is being "steadfast in the faith" and trusting in the clear presentation of the power in the death, burial and resurrection of Christ as the only solution for victory over Satanic power and influence. Paul's statement: *"We are not ignorant of his devices"* - 2 Corinthians 2:11, implies that part of Satanic strategy is to use our weaknesses to defeat us. There are several "Spiritual Dragons" that Satan employs to destroy a believer's usefulness.

When I was a student, I remember a session with a returned missionary. He went to great lengths to warn us about five of these "dragons." He said that spiritual leaders especially, as well as all believers should be aware of Satan's strategy to corrupt them in the following areas:

ON THE LOVE OF AND USE OF MONEY

Paul warns Timothy that *"they who would be rich, fall into temptation and a snare, and into many foolish and hurtful lusts, which drown men in destruction and perdition. For the love of money is the root of all evil, which while some coveted after, they have erred from the faith, and pierced themselves through with many sorrows."* - 1 Timothy 6:9-10.

How does Satan use this in the lives of believers? He uses covetousness, greed, jealousy, pride and envy in developing a spirit of discontent with their possessions. Paul shares with Timothy that *"godliness with contentment is great gain"* - 1 Timothy 6:6. The lack of contentment in one's life is the source of many fleshly lusts.

It is often a weakness pastors display when they complain about how little they are being paid. This provides for a wife and children the example that money is the reward for faithful ministry. Through the years I had to learn that it was the Lord's responsibility to support my family and me and that He would use His children to do this. Did we ever have needs? Of course! Did we always have enough money to pay our bills? No. But did the Lord provide for us in ways that we least expected? Wonderfully so! These answers to prayer bolstered our faith and reassured our dependence upon Him.

I remember one time when we went to visit our daughter and son-in-law. They were planting a church and had little assured income. My wife was watching their two little girls and said that after their naps she would have a treat for them. We began searching for food only to find that their cupboards were bare. Later, our daughter returned from "cleaning a lady's home" with a bag of groceries. We asked her if this was the only food they had and she said that the Lord had provided a house for her to clean so that she could buy some groceries. We told her that she should have called us and let us know about their need of food. Her reply was precious to us. She said "We have determined that we would tell the Lord and He will take care of us. If we had called you, daddy, we would not be living by faith." The Lord then decided to use us to go to Sam's Club and buy a trunk full of groceries. There are many other stories of the Lord's faithfulness to meet the needs of His children.

There are many accounts of men of God who were defeated in the area of the love and use of money. I have heard of situations where pastors misused the church's credit card for their own personal gain. Some Christians falsify expense accounts, cheat on their income taxes, or do not keep their word to make payments on their bills on time. The Lord allowed us to struggle at times and taught us to be careful how we used our resources. In the midst of these times of learning the Lord made His presence known through some very unusual situations.

Carol and I were married at the beginning of my senior year in college. One night we received a call from her father informing us that her mother had a heart attack and was in the hospital. Carol's little brother and sister were at home and her father asked if we could come and get them and have them stay with us for a few days. We of course agreed and drove from some distance to pick them up. On the way home I asked Carol: "What do we have to feed these kids?" She replied that we had cereal, hot dogs and beans, and some bread. We had already spent our food money for the week, and I did not get paid by my part time job until Friday. I recognized that the children needed milk but I had put the last money I had in the gas tank to go get them. Carol found a quarter in the car ash tray so we stopped at a milk machine where I intended to purchase one quart of milk. (In the 50's, dairies had milk machines much like we have soda machines today and milk was only $.25 a quart.) I deposited my quarter and pushed the selection button for one quart of milk. I still remember the sound of that quart being released and dropping into the tray at the bottom of the machine. I picked up the milk and as I was turning around, I heard another quart drop. I decided that there was no point in leaving the milk to spoil so I picked it up only to hear another quart come down the chute. Before the machine was finished, it had deposited seven quarts of milk into my hands. God had taken one quarter and multiplied it seven times! We had all the milk we needed for the rest of the week. The next week I was in the student lounge at the college I attended when men from the Board of Directors came walking through. I recognized the owner of the dairy and approached him with my story. I offered to pay him for the six extra quarts but he replied, "If God decided to give you that milk, I cannot take any money for it. God bless you, son." That was a lesson we never forgot. God illustrated to us that day that He is able to take a little and bring forth much.

A number of years ago I participated in a Direction Conference at a Christian Bible College. The conference was the project of two missions designed to provide students with the variety of ministry opportunities. During the question and answer sessions it became obvious that the interest of the students was channeled toward support schedules, retirement provisions, health insurance and other rather materialistic subjects related to their financial security. Although these are legitimate subjects and it is not wrong for prospective missionaries to ask questions about them, I was disappointed that subjects like, philosophy of ministry, doctrinal distinctives, administrative structure, missionary assignment procedures, the role of the church in the mission's program, opportunities in various areas of the world, etc, were clearly absent from most of their questions. Why this was so I can only speculate. But if creature comforts are the criteria of answering the call of God, then missions are faced with restructuring their recruiting and compensation packages to attract missionary candidates and some have done so. This can also be said about churches. Do pastors respond to a call from a church based upon how large the congregation is, how much the church will pay them, what the retirement program looks like, how much vacation can they expect, along with what other additional benefits are involved in the call? Sadly, this is often the case and churches find themselves competing for men rather than allowing the Lord to lead them in the choice.

It is true that some churches have the attitude that the pastor is an employee and that his ministry is a job and therefore they seek to "employ" him at a very basic salary. It has always been my understanding that the financial relationship between the pastor and the spiritual leaders and congregation should reflect the responsibility that the church has to support the pastor and his family by seeking to meet their needs in such a way that they do not live under financial pressure. There should be an annual evaluation and review of the pastoral package. It is a very demeaning thing when a pastor is forced to approach the spiritual leaders of the church to ask for a "raise." I have heard of churches that would go three or four years and never reconsider the pastoral package. If the church is not able to give the pastor a raise, there should be mutual consultation explaining the situation.

It is also important that a pastor avoid being in a position where he knows what people give. He should never be involved in "counting" the offering or in recording what members of his congregation give. He should not have permission to spend the Lord's money without the approval of his governing board. Expense accounts should require receipts and parameters designed to protect a pastor from accusations of extravagance or unwise expenditures. Remember, money is an arena where Satan will release his dragon to devour a man of God. Slaying that dragon through careful and powerful godly priorities in conducting one's life is of utmost importance. Contentment must be one of these priorities. When Paul gives a commentary to the Philippians on his experiences he states: *"Not that I speak in respect of want; for I have learned in whatsoever state I am, in this to be content. I know both how to be abased and I know how to abound. Everywhere and in all things I am instructed to be full and to be hungry, both to abound and to suffer need. I can do all things through Christ who strengthens me"* - Philippians 4:11-13. He then assures them in verse 19 that *"My God shall supply all your need according to His riches in glory by Christ Jesus."*

What is the guiding principle governing a spiritual leader's attitude toward money? In conversation with one of my son-in-laws before he married my daughter,

I was asked "Is it wrong for a believer to have money?" I replied "It is not wrong for a believer to have money but it is wrong for money to have the believer." Jesus challenged the rich young ruler by putting his finger on the fact that his possessions possessed him. This condition made it impossible for him to surrender them. The challenge produced sorrow in the young man and he went away full of possessions but empty in spirit.

God wants us to be willing to surrender all that we are and all that we have to Him so that He can use us in meeting ministry needs. Some time ago Carol and I were attending a Dave Ramsey Seminar. In the follow up session we were each asked to suggest something that we could forego in order to build up our "emergency fund." My mind immediately went to our regular practice of "eating out." I came from a family of nine children and it was an unusual event when we went out to eat. In spite of my wife being a good cook, I love to "eat out." So, Carol and I agreed that we were willing to give up eating out if that is what the Lord wanted. The next morning I found an envelope on my desk from a man that would not have any idea about the previous night's decision. In the envelope was five $ 50 gift certificates to restaurants in our community. He said that he felt it would be advantageous if I were to be "seen around town." Although we were willing,

God had other plans. Paul reminded the Corinthian believers that *"God is able to make all grace abound toward you, that you always having all sufficiency in all things, may abound to every good work"* - 2 Corinthians 9:8. When a believer has the right attitude toward money, he views it as a tool to do good and to further the work of the Lord. I have heard pastors say, and I agree, that all that we possess belongs to the Lord, not just our tithe. God makes us stewards of all that we possess, both time and money, and we ultimately will answer to Him as to how we have used them.

ON IMMORAL BEHAVIOR

Immoral behavior involves much more than sexual impurity. Leading a moral life includes being an example in character and integrity. It is not moral for a pastor to lie. It is not moral for a believer to be untrustworthy or for one's word to be unreliable. It is not moral for a believer to be controlled by anger, jealousy or greed. Paul includes in his list of immoral behavior " *... all uncleanness, covetousness, filthiness, foolish talking and jesting which is not convenient"* - Ephesians 5:3-5. Sexual impurity is of course soundly condemned as behavior that should not be practiced or condoned among believers. Unfortunately, sexual failure has all too often been the dragon Satan has used to bring down the ministries of spiritual leaders.

I remember talking to a well-known Bible Teacher who related to me that he had kept a little black book with the names of men who had fallen so that he could pray for them. He said the list became so long that he became discouraged and threw it away. Personally, I can name 17 men that have fallen. A spiritual leader must protect himself against the "wiles of the devil" by making wise choices. When I was a young pastor in a small church I found myself, in addition to my other duties, the youth leader. My wife is very discerning and she warned me about the intentions of one of the young ladies in the group. After one of the outings I was scheduled to take a carload of the boys home while a woman from the church was going to take the girls. When I got to my car I found this girl about which my wife had warned me, sitting in the middle in the front seat. I told her to go in the car with the girls but she refused. She wanted me to take her home last but I took her home first. In protest she refused to get out of the car. I got out and stood at the front of the car and the boys literally pushed her out. I have to admit that the boldness of this young lady scared me and when I got home I related the story to my wife and we agreed that I needed to be very careful. We decided that I would never be alone in the car with a member of the opposite sex.

Sometimes in years to come it was rather inconvenient when my wife had to take babysitters home. I adopted the same procedure concerning counseling sessions with women. I insisted that a window be installed in my office door and that someone else be in the church office. Many spiritual leaders have been falsely accused by women when there is no witness to counteract their accusations. Utilizing your wife to assist you when it is necessary to have continuing counseling sessions avoids developing an unhealthy relationship. I also found it beneficial to speak from time to time in my messages about my relationship with my wife and my deep love and appreciation for her. It lets everyone know that I am a happily married man. She always stood by my side after the services as we greeted people at the door. I remember one dear widow who waited in line to greet us. She had a serious heart problem and was sweating and when asked why she would spend the time on such a hot day waiting to see us she replied: "I just had to get my hug from Carol!"

Paul goes to great lengths to describe a man eligible for spiritual leadership as a "one woman man." Being the husband of one wife does not only mean that he is married to one woman. Implied in this statement is that he is devoted to one woman and has eyes for her only. Commenting on another woman's appearance, sexuality and beauty is not consistent with being a "one woman man." It also provides a horrible example to sons and daughters about what you appreciate in women. A man needs to model for his children what is a godly way to treat the opposite sex. As a man thinks in his heart his mouth will speak. Such comments feed lustful fantasies that eventually can become reality and expose sexual sin. I remember Dr. James Buswell saying, "You cannot keep the birds from flying around your head, but you do not have to let them build a nest in your hair." Seeking freedom from Satan's "Dragon" of impure thoughts demands that *"whatsoever things are true, whatsoever things are honest, whatsoever things are just, whatsoever things are pure, whatsoever things are lovely, whatsoever things are of good report; if there be any virtue, and if there be any praise, – that one must think on these things"* - Philippians 4:8.

Some years ago I sat down with one of the leaders of the Promise Keepers Ministry. He shared with me that one of the big problems they found among men was pornography. He related that at a recent seminar for pastors that one of the pastors stood up and with great emotion plead with the other men to pray for him because he was addicted to pornography. We all started to pray but then another pastor shared that he also was addicted. It was like someone had opened the floodgates and before it was over

60% of the pastors present had confessed to a similar addiction. Is it any wonder that pornography is such a great problem among Christian men? The addiction is so strong that it requires a strong commitment to Christ and a renewing of the mind to be loosed from this sinful practice and to be free from its corrupting influence.

A few years ago a Christian leader wrote an anonymous article in a 1992 issue of Leadership Magazine under the title "The War Within - An Anatomy of Lust" in which he recounted his journey into the depths of secret, lustful encounters with hard-core pornography. During a trip he snuck off to a bar to see a striptease show and it was downhill from there. Personally, I counseled a former youth leader in our church each Wednesday morning. His wife had given him an ultimatum and so he came to see me. He confessed that he had been involved in pornography from his days in Christian college. Each time we met together, I would ask him to look me in the eye and tell me that he had victory this last week. He had a hard time lying to me and we struggled together even though he knew that his marriage hung by a thread. Many weeks he confessed that he had fallen. I would love to tell you that he was delivered but the truth is that he continued to pursue his sexual fantasies and eventually left our church.

I have had men tell me that pornographic images will remain with you years after you believe you have had been delivered. Men need to be warned to avoid the temptation to view pornographic material because it is sin and it will have a powerful effect on their marriages, parenting and service for the Lord. Spiritual leaders need to be aware that being seduced by immoral behavior disqualifies them from active leadership. Paul reminds the Corinthians: *"I keep under my body, and bring it into subjection, lest that by any means, when I have preached to others, I myself should be a castaway"* - 1 Corinthians 9:27. Sexual sin disqualifies a man from being a pastor. One of the qualifications cited by Paul describing the qualifications of men considered for spiritual leadership is that a man be *"above reproach."* John MacArthur in his book Rediscovering Pastoral Ministry notes:

"Above reproach cannot refer to sinless perfection, because no human being could ever qualify for the office in that case, but it is a high and mature standard that speaks of being a consistent example. It is God's demand that His steward live in such a holy manner that his preaching would never be in contradiction with his lifestyle, that a pastor's indiscretions would never bring shame on the ministry, and that the shepherd's hypocrisy not undermine the flock's confidence in the ministry of God." (John MacArthur, *Rediscovering Pastoral Ministry*, p. 88)

Proverbs, discusses the seriousness of sexual sin when it states: *"But whoso commits adultery with a woman lacks understanding; he that does it destroys his own soul. A wound and dishonor shall he get; and his reproach shall not be wiped away"* - Proverbs 6:32-33. The word translated "blameless" in the list of spiritual qualifications in Titus is a negative form of *anepilemptos* meaning "to lay hold of" - Titus 1: 6-7. Sexual sin becomes a handle in a man's life that someone could "lay hold of" to accuse him of serious spiritual failure. This causes others to question his qualification to serve as a spiritual example to the Lord's flock. Paul is stating that if a man is to be placed in the office of a spiritual leader his testimony and reputation to those within and without the church must be without any legitimate ability to bring a charge against him. He must not be open to any form of censure. It is my view that spiritual leaders that have fallen into sexual sin can be restored to many opportunities to serve but they have forfeited their right to lead the church by violating their marriage covenant (if married) and the trust placed in them by God's people. I remember a Pastor of a very influential church in Bloomfield, New Jersey, saying to the pastors at an IFCA International Regional: "The reason why God places such importance on sexual sin is because it is the only area where God allows man to participate with him in the creation of life."

The Apostle Paul addresses God's response to one's rejection of His revelation of His majesty and eternal power: *"Because when they knew God they glorified him not as God, neither were thankful, but became vain in their imaginations and their foolish heart was darkened. .... they changed the glory of the incorruptible God .... Wherefore God also gave them up to uncleanness through the lust of their own hearts, to dishonor their own bodies between themselves. Who exchanged the truth of God for a lie .... For this cause God gave them up to vile affections, for even their women did exchange the natural use for that which is against nature. And likewise also the men, leaving the natural use of the woman, burned in their lust one toward another, men with men working that which is unseemly, and receiving in themselves that recompense of their error which was fitting"* - Romans 1:21-27. As America loosed itself from the Word of God and forbid any expression of the Gospel in public life, the homosexual population exploded.

ON COMPROMISING YOUR MESSAGE

Most spiritual leaders do not embark on their teaching and preaching ministries with the thought of compromising the truth. But some are lured into this trap by the Dragon of a unclear message. In the last century churches were led astray by a compromising pulpit. In this century it is the pressure from the pew that has affected the church's fidelity to the truth. Messages are often short, "needs oriented" homilies on helping people to cope with the pressures of a hectic society. Avoided are the underlying causes that manifest themselves in sinful activity. Subjects like those found in Paul's letter to the Galatian believers are avoided. Paul spoke forthrightly: *"Now the works of the flesh are manifest which are these: adultery, fornication, uncleanness, lewdness, idolatry, sorcery, hatred, contentions, outbursts of wrath, selfish ambitions, dissensions, heresies, envy, murders, revelries, and the like of which I tell you beforehand, just as I have told you in times past, that those who practice such things shall not inherit the Kingdom of God"* - Galatians 5:19-21. He was not worried about the possibility that he might offend the Galatians. In fact earlier in chapter four he stated: *"Am I, therefore, become your enemy because I tell you the truth?"* - Galatians 4:16. Because of Paul's deep concern that the Galatian believers were being deceived by those preaching another gospel, he embarked upon a detailed

banded together and were making divisive telephone calls to gather signatures on a petition to protest the unanimous decision of the elders to discipline this leader. When I finished my message I was supposed to announce disciplinary action on the leaders of the "rebellion." I had no peace to do so and waited until the benediction had been pronounced. As I began to read the statement of discipline a number of people began to walk forward in protest. The elders quickly began to write down the names of those protesting. When I finished, I walked through the group to the back of the church where I encountered a PA State Trooper. I asked him why he was there. He replied that they had heard that I was in danger and they were there to protect me. What I didn't know was that the night before a group of young men in the diner across the street were talking about forcibly removing me from the church. I asked him to please leave and he complied by parking around the side of the building to make sure nothing like what had been discussed took place. That afternoon the elders called all of those that had been a part of the protest and informed them that they were removed from any ministry until they sought to meet with the elders to explain their participation of an open protest in a worship service. There were over 1200 people there that morning and only 70 people came forward to protest. Later, one of those who marched forward told me that none of this would have happened if we had just swept the immoral behavior of the man being disciplined under the rug. We eventually lost a number of families over the action but as the years went by it was very evident that the decision of the elders to "do what was right" no matter what the consequence was the source of credibility because they were true to the responsibility placed on them by the Word of God. It would have been easy to advise the elders not to take this into the pulpit. But failing to bring to bear the Word of God upon the issue would have been derelict on our part.

Fortunately before these events were shared with the congregation, we gathered our children and shared with them that we were facing a discipline problem that could very well cost us our ministry at Limerick. We shared this with them because the decision to proceed with this discipline would also affect their lives since two of them were in college at the time. It was gratifying to hear from them "Dad, do whatever is right, be assured that we are behind you."

Those were trying days and I remember slipping off by myself and going to the mountains for a time of uninterrupted prayer and reflection. I am not a poet, but I remember sitting down at the desk in my room and penning these words.

ASSURANCE

In the quietness of my closet
My heart has found its rest
For the blessing of Thy Word
Did satisfy my quest

For the surety of Thy favor
And the warmth of Thy desire
Came flooding slowly o'er me
As a glowing, growing fire.

The doubts and fears of failure
Began to ebb away
As the certainty of my calling
Was renewed for me that day.

With confidence and boldness
I rose up from my knees
To provide the godly leader's cup
With only my Savior to please.

For the One who stands beside me
Requires at my hand
That His steward be found faithful
To the will of His command.

What comes my way tomorrow
Is none of my concern
For He asks me to be steadfast
'Till the day of His return.

Tomorrow's ills and trials
Are fully in His hand
So I'll not fret or worry
But simply take my stand

Upon the truth, the Word of God
Which warms my heart anew
And promises His faithfulness
Will always bring me through.

So Spirit of the living God
Examine all my way
Forgive and cleanse my sinful self
And use me God today

Richard Gregory - 1979

ON DISCIPLINING OUT OF A HEART OF LOVE

It seems like whenever the church exercises discipline those opposed to the action will always say: "It wasn't exercised correctly. It wasn't loving." Christian love does not mean toleration but it requires loving confrontation. Many are not willing to do this because it is both uncomfortable and means that the searchlight will be turned on them. Paul tells us that *"when a brother is overtaken in a fault, you who are spiritual restore such a one in the spirit of meekness, considering yourself lest you also be tempted"* - Galatians 6:1. Spiritual leadership must be spiritually qualified in order to pursue discipline in a manner that fulfills the biblical mandate. Be assured that if there are areas of their own lives that are spiritually deficient, Satan will see to it that they are exposed. There are five basic reasons why God has given us the responsibility to pursue discipline when someone is living in sin:

a. To restore a sinning brother or sister to fellowship with the Lord and His people - Galatians 6:1
b. To be obedient to the Word of God and therefore maintain the purity of the church and stay the removal of God's blessing - 1 Timothy 1:18-20
c. To give the congregation the opportunity to reach out to the sinning person urging him/her to repent - Matthew 18:15-17

d. To exemplify to all that the church is serious about discipline in order that others may fear - 1 Timothy 5:19-20
e. Ultimately when the church is obedient it brings glory to God - 1 Corinthians 10:31

I remember one incident when a pastor called me to meet with his deacons on a matter of discipline. The youth pastor had been caught downloading pornographic material on the church's computer. The youth pastor confessed and asked the deacons for forgiveness. Some felt that was all that we required. When I approached the discussion of the qualification in 1 Timothy 3 and Titus 1 one of the deacons commented "Those are only suggestions as guidelines. No one can meet all those requirements." I knew right then and there that I was dealing with men that did not understand the proper application of Scripture and no amount of reasoning or teaching was going to alter this. They did not want their congregation to know of the incident and were therefore going to sweep it under the rug and let the youth pastor continue in his position. I then asked them if they felt that this would be the best for the youth pastor? Did they believe that he was spiritually strong enough to be on the "point" in the spiritual battle for their youth? I reminded them that he will be in Satan's cross hairs and therefore needs some time to prove that he is winning this battle. I went away with little hope that the church would survive without major spiritual loss. A short time later the pastor left.

ON RELYING ON METHODS

There is an approach to ministry that is described as "Jesuit Casuistry." Simply stated it means the end justifies the means. The radical application of this approach says that it is alright to lie if you reserve the truth in your mind and if you have a good reason for lying. It also means that you can knowingly violate scripture if good is accomplished. I suppose a good illustration of this occurs in mass evangelism when liberal and unbelieving clergy are invited to participate as sponsors in order to get their congregations to attend. Unholy alliances are forged in order to reach the most people with the gospel. Although this may seem noble to some the scripture teaches that *"obedience is better than sacrifice."* 1 Samuel 15:22

Methods are not wrong. We all use some methods to communicate the gospel. However, some methods do not glorify God, especially when they mimic the world in its quest to control people. I remember being in a Christian bookstore and seeing a display of "Christian Music" advertising a group called "Sheep in Wolves Clothing." Their picture mirrored an acid rock band. I am sure that their motive was pure but their message was compromised by their methods. There is a great danger that the church will use methods to attract people that do not reflect real devotion to Christ. One Sunday morning I was scheduled to preach in two different churches about a mile apart. When I finished preaching in one church I had enough time to get to the other in time to preach there. I waited patiently as the "band" did its thing taking up about 45 minutes of time leaving me less than 15 minutes to speak. When the band finished, they left the church and I could see them outside smoking and having a good old time. It appeared that they had no interest in hearing the Word. I quickly greeted the people, shared a verse and then had to rush off to the other church to be on time for its service. It is hard for me to understand how spiritual leadership in that church could both promote and use these young men in that band in its worship service. However, it might be that they felt that if they used them they could reach them. Was their offering to the Lord acceptable? Did not Paul identify what was our *"reasonable service"* in Romans 12:1-2 It is the responsibility of spiritual leaders to guard the worship service and keep it Christ centered rather than man centered entertainment.

Some methods appeal to the basic needs of people. People like to be rewarded. So some methods used by churches are centered on rewarding people for riding their bus, attending their youth group, etc. This teaches people to serve because of the benefits and not out of love. The Church at Ephesus is a prime example of this. John speaks for the Lord when he writes in Revelation 2:2-3 *"I know your works and your labor and your patience and how you cannot bear them who are evil; and you have tried them that say they are apostles, and are not, and has found them liars; you have borne and have patience and for my name's sake have labored and have not fainted"* Their methods of service were all exemplary but unacceptable because they had left their first love. They had turned away from serving because of love and were serving for some other reason. They were warned to repent and return to their original purpose for serving, purely out of love for the Lord. Churches that order their worship services around entertaining men and not around exalting Christ have succumbed to the Dragon of Unacceptable Methods that produce counterfeit worship.

ON HIDDEN MOTIVES

The scripture warns us that our *"hearts are deceitful and desperately wicked"* - Jeremiah 17:9. God's servants need to constantly check what the real desires of their hearts are. Often their motives are hidden even from them. But sooner or later believers will discern selfish motives and will lose trust and respect for leaders with hidden motives. One of the most common illustrations of this occurs when a pastor is candidating for a church and there are things that he either disagrees with or that do not meet his preferences. He proceeds to accept the church's call with the hidden intention of changing those things in the future when his leadership base is established. Later when his true intentions are exposed, the church loses its trust in him and his integrity is compromised. Transparency is of the utmost importance in a leader's motives.

Recently, I did a short term pastorate in the church where I grew up. In meeting with the Elders I noted that there were several basic issues in the constitution that needed attention and if I became the pastor I would attempt to address them. I pointed out that there was a contradiction between the doctrinal statement and the requirements for membership. This was the same problem I faced some 40 years before when coming to Limerick Chapel. The doctrinal statement had a clear presentation of the doctrine of baptism describing that immersion of believers was the only baptism recognized. The membership section required that a person be in agreement with the doctrinal statement without reservation. It then went on to say that baptism was not required for membership. This was an obvious contradiction.

Also, the church's name was the source of some confusion. Although when the name Gospel Tabernacle was first used it reflected the ministry of the North Side Gospel Tabernacle in Chicago, which was a popular church with Moody students in the 1940's. Later it was being used by many charismatic churches. The church received numerous calls asking us if we were Four Square, Pentecostal or some other branch of the Charismatic Movement. Several attempts had tried to change the name but could not get the support needed from the members. So I set about the task carefully and prayerfully. After being at the church for a year, I mentioned to the congregation that there were several problems with our documents.

One thing missing was a disciplinary procedure without which a church is subject to legal action if discipline of a member were necessary. I asked that a committee be appointed to study our documents and make appropriate recommendations to improve them. They readily agreed and the committee was called Constitutional Revision Committee. They met for over a year. During this time I kept the congregation informed of what was being considered for revision and the reasoning behind the consideration. I also explained how the church's name did not reflect who we are and what we believed. Transparency was the key in helping the congregation understand the process.

Two weeks before the church's annual meeting, a document was given to each of the members showing each change in contrast to the original text. The church's boards had agreed to also present a recommendation to change the name to Tabernacle Bible Church. The night of the meeting each change was presented individually and projected on one of the two screens along with the original text on the other. Members were given the opportunity to question, comment and ask for a vote on each change. If no vote was called for, we went on to the next recommended change. Over 40 changes were presented with no one calling for a vote on any individual change. We then voted on the recommendations as whole. By the grace of God, the recommended changes were adopted with a unanimous vote. We then brought up the recommended name change. There was much discussion and finally the question was called for and the name of Tabernacle Bible Church was adopted with a 93% vote. A number of those voting "no" said they did so because they preferred Honesdale be included in the name not because they opposed changing the name. There were no hidden motives in the actions of the Constitutional Revision Committee or by me as the pastor. Change was accomplished and unity was maintained.

CHAPTER SEVEN

How Do I Preach with Power?

I n Ephesians 4:11-12, the Apostle Paul shared the truth that the Lord Jesus gave gifts to the church. They included apostles, prophets, evangelists, pastors and teachers. These gifted men were given the responsibility of equipping the saints for the work of the ministry and the edifying of the body of Christ. They did so through the declaration of the Word of God. Evangelists, pastors and teachers are especially important in the church today. Jeremiah lived in a day when God's people were living evil lives. He described his day as characterized by: *"You defiled my land and made my heritage an abomination. The priest said not, 'Where is the Lord' and they that handle the law knew me not. The rulers also transgressed against me and the prophets prophesied by Baal and walked after things that do not profit. Hath a nation changed their gods which are yet no gods? But my people have changed their glory for that which does not profit.*" - Jeremiah 1:7-8 &11. Israel was guilty of turning away from the Lord to other gods; they had presented their children as a human sacrifices - Jeremiah 2:34; they had desecrated marriage through divorcing their wives; and they refused to admit that they had sinned. This was the generation that Jeremiah was called to shepherd. His message was clear: *"Turn, O backsliding children, saith the Lord; for I am married to you and I will take you one of a city, and two of a family and I will bring you to Zion"* - Jeremiah 3:14. His promise to a repentant people was that God would bless them: *"I will give you shepherds according to my heart, who shall feed you with knowledge and understanding"* - Jeremiah 3:15. In comparing this promise to Israel with the promise in Ephesians 4:11-12 and you get the New Testament equivalent of the shepherding ministry given to Israel: godly men equipped to shepherd the church in the midst of an evil society.

ON SHEPHERDS BEING A GIFT
FROM GOD TO THE CHURCH

The certainty of a Call is essential to an understanding of the role of a shepherd in the life of the church. It is not a choice but a response to the hand of God on one's life. Paul sites this when he says" *"I am appointed a preacher, and an apostle, and a teacher of the Gentiles"* - 2 Timothy 1:11. He shares with Timothy*: "And I thank Christ Jesus, our Lord, who has enabled me in that he counted me faithful, putting me into the ministry"* - 1 Timothy 1:12. The writer of the Hebrews in describing how the High Priest was chosen and ordained noted that *"no man takes this honor unto himself, but he that is called of God as was Aaron"* - Hebrews 5:1-4.

Through the years I have known men who began preparation for the ministry but in the midst they realized that they had no certainty of a call from God. I have always advised men not to enter the pastorate as an experiment, thinking that if they were not successful or did not enjoy it, they could try some other pursuit. If shepherds are a gift of God to the church it is a sacred responsibility to be subject to the Giver.

God's promise to Israel concerning His gifts of shepherds included a description of their ministry.

1. THEY WOULD BE MEN ACCORDING TO MY OWN HEART. (JEREMIAH 3:15)

Men who have the heart of the Lord will reflect those things of which God is passionate. They will be interested in a holy life. They would be characterized by grace and mercy. They would be eager to be forgiving.

They would exhibit godly love. They would always seek peace. Their joy in the Lord would be constant and evident. They would not give up easily in seeking to bring men to conformity to Christ and have victory over sin. Their gentleness, goodness, temperance and meekness would be spoken of as that which were the ornaments of their personal lives and ministry.

This challenge is great and means that a primary responsibility of a man of God is to guard his own heart and dedicate every day to being Christ-like in all his attitudes and actions. He must make sure that his ministry of the word is filtered first through his own heart before it is presented to God's people. The humility of being dependent upon the power of the Spirit is necessary to powerful preaching.

2. THEY WILL FEED THE LORD'S FLOCK

In Psalm 23, the Shepherd's Psalm, the sheep under the shepherd's care are led into green pastures, beside still waters and in paths of righteousness. The shepherd will cause the sheep to get the proper rest and cause them to rest at noon (Song of Solomon 1:7). Making sure that God's sheep are fed a balanced diet requires a preaching plan that is balanced and addresses the great doctrines of the Word and then applies them to daily living.

3. THEY WILL FEED THE LORD'S FLOCK
WITH KNOWLEDGE

AWANA has a very good verse to explain their goals: *"Study to show thyself approved unto God, a workman that needs not to be ashamed, rightly dividing the Word of Truth"* - 2 Timothy 2:15. The word *"study"* here means to invest oneself, which seems to indicate hard work. It is hard work to mine the "gold" out of the Word so that you can feed the flock with meat not milk. My recommendation is that one's approach to preaching should be expository which requires extensive study of the text exegetically, historically and etymologically. Many use the topical approach which lends itself to narrative preaching which is heavily slanted toward a needs-oriented application. A theological foundation is often neglected in this approach. As one preacher in describing this approach calls it "Sermonettes for Christianettes." You cannot share what you do not know and knowledge of the Word of God requires hard work. Powerful preaching feeds God's flock and they are healthy.

4. THEY WILL FEED THE FLOCK
WITH UNDERSTANDING.

Understanding the needs of the flock demands that you know them as individuals. The sheep need to feel that they are a part of the flock and not an outsider looking in. This is often hard to accomplish if the church is large and growing. Integrating people into smaller groups is one answer. Having aggressively recruiting Sunday School classes is a way of providing an arena in which a person can identify with others in the congregation. Making sure that there are groups that are designed to encourage people having particular problems or needs in mind, such as going through a divorce, struggling with problems of homosexuality, troubled marriages, rebellious children, addiction, and abuse. We can think that these things do not occur in our congregations, but my experience is that do. Knowing how to take people to the Word of God in counseling in such situations illustrates feeding people with understanding. Powerful preaching demands both understanding of the Word and God's people.

Powerful preaching depends upon the vessel used of God being filled with the Holy Spirit. Great oratory can be accomplished by mere talent but the powerful presentation of the truth understood by the human heart is only through the uninhibited ministry of the Holy Spirit. May God in His graciousness grant each of His servants the humility to recognize this truth and may each one guard his own soul from pride, self-sufficiency, and presumption.

CHAPTER EIGHT

How Do I Respond in Time of Crisis?

read recently of some research done among 450 ministers concerning what they thought were the most common crises they faced in their ministries. The survey revealed the nine most prevalent crises faced among the people of their congregations. The nine in descending order of difficulty are: domestic violence/family abuse, suicide, homosexuality, death of a child, drug/alcohol abuse, divorce, adultery/sexual misconduct, death of a spouse and catastrophic/terminal illness. (James D, Berkley, *Called into Crisis* (Carol Stream, Illinois) Christianity Today and Word Inc, 1989, p 11.) In over fifty years of ministry I have faced them all, along with several others. It would be nice to be able to say that there were pat answers to overcome the tragic results of being overtaken in a crisis that shakes one's faith. What is important is that a pastor and/or spiritual leader be tender, caring, understanding with a genuine love for the believer that finds himself/herself faced with decisions and consequences one would not naturally choose. The careful application of the Word of God is of utmost importance.

ON WEEPING WITH THOSE WHO WEEP

It was one o'clock in the morning when I awoke to the telephone ringing. A call at that time of the morning usually means something bad has happened. The father on the line said, "Our son has just been killed in a car accident." He told me that he was at Grandview Hospital but another one of our teen-age boys had been taken by helicopter to Allentown. Carol and I quickly dressed, called my assistant pastor, David Jones, to meet me at Grandview Hospital. When Carol and I arrived we embraced the grieving parents and prayed with them for the strength of God's grace. Soon my assistant pastor arrived and Carol and I left for the hospital in Allentown. We arrived just as the Doctor was telling the parents that he could not save their son. We cried together. I would spend many hours with those two couples over the next several months. They needed to know that Carol and I really loved them and understood as best we could their hurt and grief. It was important that I did not use trite phrases and platitudes often used by people to endeavor to comfort when tragic death has occurred.

This was brought home to me recently when I met a friend in a restaurant. His wife had died while I was ministering in Pennsylvania and this was the first time that I had seen him. I reached out and gave him a hug and he said "I miss her so." They had been married for fifty years and their lives were intertwined. I said "I know that you loved her very much. God loves her too and He will take care of her for you until you join her." He thanked me for not giving him a pat answer. He shared how some had tried to comfort him by saying "She's in a better place now." Although their intention was good, it came across to him as if he had not taken good care of her. He still felt that the best place for her was at his side. He thanked me profusely and told all of our mutual friends that I had helped him understand his feelings surrounding his wife's death. We are aware that only the grace of God gives us the words to share at times like these.

Other crises experienced in our many years of ministry included receiving a call from the police in West Virginia asking me to go to the home of one of our young men who had drowned on a cave exploring expedition. I had to call and ask the parents' permission to come to their home at 11:00 PM to share the tragic news with them. This was especially difficult since I was new at the church and had not established a close relationship with them.

On another occasion, someone came into our backyard where we were having a 4th of July picnic, yelling, "Jimmy is down in the river." A family in the church had gone down to the Susquehanna River for a picnic and their two boys had gone swimming. The oldest boy got in trouble and drowned. When I got there, the mother was so distraught that I saw right away that she was going to need a sedative. Being there at times like these affords one the opportunity to comfort with the Word of God and prayer. Being available in the succeeding days is also of the utmost importance. Showing genuine love is a comfort in itself. I have found that when death comes to a family that your continuing ministry is often most important several weeks after when family has dispersed and ones grieving finds themselves alone.

We had just visited a dear friend of ours in Southern California and they shared with us that their daughter and her husband were on a fall foliage trip to New England. That is always a very beautiful time of year in the northeast and we rejoiced with them. Shortly after we left to travel to northern California we received a call from our friend Delbert. In the background I could hear wailing. He said that their daughter had been in a horrible accident and wasn't expected to live. Anna was hysterical and he couldn't get her calmed down. I asked him to put her on the phone. She was still wailing when I said to her in a firm voice, "Anna, be quiet, I am going to pray." Immediately she became quiet and as I prayed she later testified that the Lord brought a sweeping calmness over her that gave her assurance that the Lord was in control. Prayer was the key to quietness. They traveled to Boston to be with their daughter who, by the way, recovered. Glory to God for His powerful demonstration of His presence during the time of this crisis.

ON DEALING WITH PERSONAL CRISES

It is one thing to be there to minister to others who are going through a crisis, but how about when the crisis comes to you personally. Carol and I were in California when I received a call from our youngest daughter, Cynthia. "Daddy, they just told us that Josalyn is profoundly deaf." Josalyn was our 18 month old granddaughter who had successfully "fooled" all of us because she was so perceptive.

The news devastated us and we quickly flew home to be with our daughter and her husband. I knew little about deafness but my limited knowledge caused me to conclude that her future was bleak. Sunday found us in our church at Byron Center where our son was pastor. He had picked our favorite songs, but I found that I could not sing without breaking into tears.

After the service we went to Tim and Cynthia's home for dinner. As we sat at the table I asked "How are you doing?" to which they replied, "We're OK - but how about you, Dad?" I broke into tears and Josalyn, who was sitting in the high chair next to me, climbed down, climbed up on my lap and began to wipe away my tears with my napkin. Needless to say, my weeping continued. My heart was broken and I could not "feel" the presence of God. As I processed this, I was led to write the following article for the Voice. At the time, I was somewhat reluctant to share this very personal perspective. I called Elwood Chipchase who was president of the IFCA International at the time. I shared with him the article and he urged me to include it in the Voice Magazine. He noted "that the Article would give our membership a glance at another side of you that many had never seen. There are many men that have had the same feelings that you had." The following article appeared in the Voice Magazine in the January/February Issue.

FAITHFULNESS

Standing to my feet as the final strains of the organist's introduction filled my ears. I had a lump in my throat and I found that every time I tried to sing, I started to cry. Near me believers were reverently singing "Great is thy Faithfulness, Oh God my Father..." I wanted to join them and shout it from my heart, but all I could do was bow my head and pray. I was experiencing emotions I didn't know how to handle. I was facing an uncertain future with a darling granddaughter that was special to her grandmother and me. You see, we had just found out that Josalyn, our 18 month old granddaughter, was deaf. I hurt for Tim and Cindy. I hurt for Josalyn. I hurt for Carol. I hurt for myself. I didn't know much about deafness. I knew that people that were severely hearing impaired often could not speak. It was the lack of articulation that first caused us to wonder whether Josalyn had a hearing problem. But she was extremely visual and communicative with her gestures and facial expressions. She waved, she laughed, she pointed and her intelligence and personality circumvented her inability to hear. But now we knew and I hurt in spite of my knowledge of God's faithfulness. Would Cindy ever hear her say "mommy?" Would that bright little mind ever grasp the wonders of ideas and delve into the complexities of the mass of information

emotions and a frustrating feeling of helpless-
ness. Only then did the healing process begin.

It occurred to me as I thought on these things,
that many people with hurts far deeper than
mine had been under my ministry through
the years. It was very probable that they, like
I, had sat in our services, empty, hurting,
and crying inside. Words did not help, but
just being with the people of God did. I was
reminded of the words of Paul in **Hebrews
10:23-25** *"Let us hold fast the confession of our
hope without wavering, for He who promised is
faithful; and let us consider how to stimulate one
another to love and good deeds, not forsaking our
own assembling together, as is the habit of some,
but encouraging one another, and so much the more
as you see the day drawing near."* God's people,
being together provide the framework for
encouragement. God's people reaching out to
one another in sensitive understanding provide the oil of comfort in the healing process.
The ministry of the Holy Spirit, so needed
when one is hurting, is realized through the
presence of another believer. How often did
I go to be with someone in grief, not knowing what to say, and saying very little, only
to have them share with me later that just my

saith my soul; therefore will I hope in Him. The Lord is good unto them that wait for Him, to the soul that seeketh Him. It is good that a man should hope and quietly wait for the Lord" - Lamentations 3:22-26. Because of the goodness of my God, my hurts did not turn into bitterness. My disappointment has become opportunity and my fears the fuel for the Holy Spirit's healing work in my life. Now when I sing "Great is Thy faithfulness, oh God my Father ..." I remember that God is faithful even when my hurt keeps me from feeling it.

Voice - January/February 1995

Now let me tell you the rest of the story. Tim and Cynthia had three more children, two of them suffering the same deafness. Before the children were born, Tim had written a research paper for a class on "Children with Special Needs." He chose to write on "Children with Deafness" and they were thus prepared with the knowledge needed to make decisions on the road to take in their children's education. They chose to pursue having cochlear implants and teaching their children to speak. It was helpful that both Tim and Cynthia were teachers and Cynthia became deeply involved in the Hearing Impaired Program in Kent County. She became an advocate for the children in the special Hearing Impaired School when there was an attempt to mainstream them. It was a lot of hard work and demanded a lot of their time. But today, Josalyn is a sophomore at Bob Jones University and speaks fluently with almost no evidence of her hearing impairment. Lindsay is a senior at Bob Jones Academy, is an honor student and is also very articulate. Drew, their youngest is a freshman at Bob Jones Academy is doing well and has proved to be a hard worker. The road was long and tough, but God proved Himself faithful every step of the way. Their one hearing daughter, Kayla, is a freshman at Bob Jones University. She has faithfully ministered to her siblings and has been an encouragement to them when times were tough. Her experiences have prepared her to minister to others in the years to come.

I learned much about ministering to those in crisis by going through one myself. God has a way of preparing us through our experiences to be able to share God's care and faithfulness to others. Paul points to this when he shares with the Corinthians: *"Blessed be God even the Father of our Lord Jesus Christ, the Father of mercies, and the God of all comfort, who comforts us in all our tribulation, that we may be able to comfort them who are in any trouble with that which we ourselves are comforted of God"*

- 2 Corinthians 1:3-4. I am sure that Peter spoke from experience when encouraging believers suffering persecution when he said *"Casting all your care upon Him for he cares for you"* - 1 Peter 5:7.

These children have brought such joy to our whole family. They have achieved much through their faithful dedication. When we attended Josalyn's High School graduation my heart swelled with gratefulness to God for His faithfulness. Robed in her honors colors and ranking 12th in a class of 251 she was a walking illustration of the faithfulness of our Heavenly Father's love and care.

CHAPTER NINE

How Do I Emphasize the Importance of Prayer in the Life of the Church?

E veryone knows that prayer is very important in God's plan. We are commanded to *"pray without ceasing"* - 1 Thessalonians 5:17. Jesus spent all night in prayer before choosing His apostles and agonized in prayer in the garden before His crucifixion. Those of us committed to the sovereignty of God often struggle in our attempt to understand how prayer changes things. Somehow we know that it changes the one praying. Personally I simply accept the fact that *"the secret things belong unto the Lord our God"* - Deuteronomy 29:29. Paul asks the Roman Christians to *"agonize together with me in your prayers to God for me"* - Romans 15:30. He requests that the Ephesian Christians be *"praying always with all prayer and supplications in the Spirit, and watching thereunto with all perseverance and supplication for all saints, and for me that utterance may be given unto me that I may open my mouth boldly, that I may make known the mystery of the gospel for which I am an ambassador in bonds, that therein I may speak boldly as I ought to speak"* -Ephesians 6:18-20. Can we afford to minimize it in our ministries?

ON STAFF PRAYER

The tremendous effect prayer has on a ministry was brought home to me when I joined the staff at Limerick Chapel. The staff had a Monday morning prayer meeting during which we prayed for a number of people listed in a book. When someone came to Christ, the date was entered beside his or her name. As I looked through the book there was a large number of people listed that had trusted Christ. I joined the staff on August 8, 1970 and on that first Monday I prayed for Marty and Fran McCormick. Marty was a staunch Roman Catholic. He and his wife had been visited by the Jehovah's Witness and they went next door to visit Fred and Kay Tinkler to ask questions. Through the influence of the Tinklers, Marty came to know the Lord. I remember the date well, it was August 16th. I was able to write "Saved – August 16" beside his name at the following staff prayer meeting. God used Marty in a wonderful way at the Chapel. He had a hunger for the Word and enrolled in PCB's night school. He became a deacon and then an elder. He chaired our building committee when we built a large addition to the Chapel. Most important to me, he was an evidence of the result of the faithful prayers of our pastoral staff.

ON REGULAR PRAYER MEETINGS

Each Saturday night the Chapel held a prayer meeting. Our Elders were divided into four groups and assigned one Saturday night a month to be present and lead a group. An extensive list of prayer requests was distributed. People of the congregation were urged to choose a Saturday night and endeavor to be present to wait on the Lord. One very important item on the prayer list was the services that would take place the next day. We would pray that the Word of God would have free course and impact the lives of those attending. I endeavored to take our children to that prayer meeting and they have testified that they learned much about prayer as they prayed with some of the older saints. Our missionaries, servicemen, students and sick were all held up before the Lord in that prayer meeting.

Although the elders were not "required" to come each Saturday night, I felt that I should endeavor to be there as a testimony of the importance of the "Church at Prayer." In addition to the Saturday night prayer meeting, Missions Prayer Groups met each Sunday night before the evening service. There were the Africa Prayer Group, the South American Prayer Group, the Jewish Prayer Group, the European Prayer Group that met on successive weeks. Each group prayed for and corresponded with our missionaries in its particular area of the world and often received offerings to help with particular projects. Missions were a very important part of the ministry of the Chapel.

Although we were very missionary minded, I felt that we had not targeted one of the areas that defined a "Mission Minded Church." I remember preaching in a famous missionary church in Canada that was noted for its missionary giving. The church gave a lot from its resources but produced very little in sending missionaries from its membership. The text of my sermon that night was "Pray ye therefore, the Lord of the harvest that he will send forth reapers into His harvest." I came home and did some evaluation of our own missions program and realized that relatively few of our people had responded to the call of God to missions.

We were supporting "the fruit of other ministries" but growing very little fruit of our own. I called upon the congregation to join me in praying that God would raise up twenty young people to hear the call of God to vocational ministry. We faithfully pursued that goal and when I left the Chapel seventeen years later they told me that sixty young people had entered into vocational ministry. We prayed, God answered and to Him goes all the glory. Years later I became the pastor of my home church in Honesdale, Pennsylvania. I found a similar condition – money but not missionaries. The missions committee got the vision and the church adopted a motto: "Ten from the Tabernacle." We began to see young people respond and already several are in the pipeline preparing to be missionaries.

ON PRAYER FOR THE PULPIT MINISTRY

Prayer is essential in preparing the heart of a pastor before he goes into the pulpit to open the Word of God. One should pray over the text asking the Lord to instill it into his heart. Prayer should include those that will hear that the Lord will bring conviction and repentance where sin is present, comfort and peace where it is needed and encouragement to those prone to discouragement. Early each Sunday morning I would go to the church and walk up and down the aisles praying for the people that would soon occupy those pews. I knew where they would be sitting and if I knew of a special need I would bring it before the Lord. When I entered the pulpit that morning, I knew I had prepared my heart to be a messenger of the Lord in teaching the truths of God's Word and bringing them to bear on the issues of life. Through prayer I had given the Lord the opportunity to instill the message into my heart so that in the preaching the Spirit of God would reach hearts. It has been said that messages that come from the head reach heads, but messages that come from the heart reach hearts. If I missed that prayerful preparation, I could feel it.

One Sunday during a very difficult time in the life of the church, one of the elders came to me and said that he and several other members would not be in the worship service because they were going to gather in my study and pray for me while I was preaching. I was delighted to hear this and encouraged him to organize several prayer teams to pray on assigned Sundays. From that day forward, I enjoyed the prayer support of a good number of men. I knew they were praying while I was preaching. When we came to Florida I shared this concept with our pastor and presently there are six prayer teams that pray on assigned Sunday's for him. For many years I was privileged to be a part of one of those teams.

ON THE IMPORTANCE OF PRAYER

It is very important to be careful not to minimize the importance of prayer. A pastor needs to teach his congregation to pray. When a very important decision in the life of the church is required, spiritual leadership should call for a day of prayer when the church can come before the Lord seeking His guidance. I received much guidance from a little book *"Method in Prayer"* by Scroggie. In this book he divides the prayer life into five categories. He suggests that we balance our prayers to include the following categories: Adoration; Confession; Thanksgiving; Intercession and Petition. Satan goes to all ends to keep the church off its knees or to focus our prayer lives on our own needs. There is great power in a balanced prayer life including pleading with our Heavenly Father to compel His children to enter the harvest. Men seem to become what they are praying about. Men cannot sincerely plead with God and then walk away without saying "Here am I, Lord send me." We are instructed by the Apostle Paul to *"Pray without ceasing"* - 1 Thessalonians 5:17. Jesus taught that *"Men ought always to pray and not faint"* - Luke 18:1. If Jesus thought that prayer was important how can the church order its program without dependence on the prayers of God's people. The church needs to pray regularly for its pastor, elders, deacons and missionaries. As a pastor and his wife, we prayed daily for our children. We also prayed for the person they were going to marry that God would keep them pure and urged our children to do likewise. A church genuinely given to prayer is a mighty power for God.

ON THE BIBLICAL MODEL FOR PRAYER

Prayer is not only putting our thoughts into words, it is an attitude of dependence upon the work of grace in our hearts and the hearts of others. It is an instrument that the Lord uses to unify the saints in the progress of the Gospel. Paul reaches out to the Roman Christians and pleads with them *"to strive (Greek: agonize) together with me in your prayers to God for me; that I may be delivered from them that do not believe in Judea; and that my service which I have for Jerusalem may be accepted of the saints; and that I may come unto you with joy by the will of God, and may with you be refreshed"* - Romans 15:30-33. He knew how important the prayers of the saints are. In writing to the church at Ephesus he placed prayer as the capstone of the armor needed to successfully stand against the wiles of the Devil. He instructed the church to be *"praying always with all prayer and supplication in the Spirit, and watching thereunto with all perseverance and supplication for all saints; and for me, that utterance may be given unto me, that I may open my mouth boldly, to make known the mystery of the gospel"* - Ephesians 6:18-19. And finally in writing to the church at Thessalonica: *"Brethren, pray for us, that the Word of the Lord may have free course and be glorified even as it is with you; and that we may be delivered from unreasonable and wicked men; for all men have not faith"* - 2 Thessalonians 3:1-2.

If prayer was not important in the process of the Gospel and the protection of God's servants, the Holy Spirit would never have moved in the heart of Paul to call upon the saints for this support. Prayer opens the channel of God's provision and protection as we stand shoulder to shoulder with the saints. Samuel realized this when speaking to God's people: *"For God will not forsake His people for His great name's sake, for it hath pleased the Lord to make you His people, Moreover, as for me, God forbid that I should sin against the Lord by ceasing to pray for you"* - 1 Samuel 12:22-23. Prayer is a ministry. It is a dedication to service. It is an integral ingredient of spiritual maturity. Paul concludes his instruction to the Thessalonians by instructing them *"to pray without ceasing"* and *"Brethren, pray for us"* - 1 Thessalonians 5:17 & 25. Finally, Paul included *"praying always. ... for all saints.... and for me"* in the armor in Ephesians 6.

CHAPTER TEN

How Do I Avoid the Danger of Leaving "Your First Love?"

I t seems like the church at Ephesus was doing all the right things. It was commended for its faithful service, its tireless love and careful discernment. Yet with all its activity and careful planning, it fell short in a very essential dimension of the life of the church. It was doing all the right things but with the wrong motivation. It was devoted to the "church" but had turned its attention to the mechanics of the ministry rather than serving from a heart of love for the Lord. John records the words of Jesus: *"Nevertheless, I have somewhat against you because you have left your first love."* What an indictment coming from the lips of the Lord of the Church. This verse is often quoted "You have lost your first love" but the word *"left"* seems to indicate a change in focus from loving the Lord to "using the Lord in ministry." The Lord calls the church to repentance and warns of the consequence of failure to do so.

Although planning, programs and personnel are essential to growing the church, they can also become substitutes for genuine dependence upon the empowering presence of the Holy Spirit. Love for the Lord is recognizing total dependence on and devotion to the Lord of the Church in serving God acceptably.

ON THE DECEPTION OF THE CULTURE

Today, many view the church through the lens of culture. Although culture cannot be totally ignored, it must never dictate adjustment of the truth to accommodate either the presentation or content of the Gospel. The church is called upon to minister within the culture but never upon the culture. There is a movement today called "the Emergent Church" that has adjusted the authority of Scripture in determining truth and has concluded that truth is relative and subject to the refinement of the prevalent culture. The result is the shift in emphasis in worship from a God centered worship to the needs of men. A needs-oriented worship service will often emphasize pleasing the people with the music of their culture and short homilies about human problems. Exegesis of Scripture is too "heavy" or "authoritative" for immature Christians and so it is abandoned.

What is the consequence of ignoring the authority of Scripture in determining truth? Experience, emotion and expression become the ground of truth and faith becomes man-centered and thus very relative. Worship becomes entertainment and God is relegated to the sidelines to be substituted as needed. Scripture becomes a guideline and cannot be taken literally. "True truth" as Francis Schaeffer calls it, is hidden from discovery and theology becomes a divisive tool in the hands of those out of touch with reality.

ON UNDERSTANDING BIBLICAL LOVE

Love in the minds of some is relative and is therefore often characterized by feeling. Biblical love, "agape," involves "the recognition of intrinsic value." Recognizing the finished work of Christ as the ground of salvation results in confidence in the promises of God as revealed in an authoritative, errorless Scripture. One's salvation depends upon the integrity of God and not the faithfulness of man. Genuine love for the Lord is *"spread abroad in ones heart by the Holy Spirit"* – Romans 5:5. *"For the fruit of the Spirit is love, joy, peace, longsuffering, gentleness, goodness, faith, meekness, temperance: against such there is no law"* -Galatians 5:22.

Love for the Lord is the motivating factor in obedience. Jesus said *"If you keep my commandments ye shall abide in my love"* - John 15:10. There are some that obey the Lord out of fear of the consequences of disobedience. I remember one dear lady who told me that she wished she could believe in the security of the believer, because there are a lot of things she would love to do, but was afraid to do them. A love-centered relationship with the Lord is not a self-centered relationship. It is not what we receive in our salvation that really counts, it is the knowledge that we have been purchased with the price of the blood of Christ that brings confidence and strength to our faith. *"We love Him because He first loved us"* - 1 John 4:19. The realization of the genuine love of God becomes the pattern of our expression of that love for brothers and sisters in our spiritual family. *"Hereby perceive we the love of God, because He laid down His life for us: and we ought to lay down our lives for the brethren"* - 1 John 3:16.

ON TESTING YOUR LOVE

Of a Pastor for the Lord's flock.

It is difficult to evaluate yourself with respect to whether or not your expressions of love are genuine. Words are not enough. Jesus pointed out that *"They praise me with their lips but their hearts are far from me."* There are some questions a man can ask himself to evaluate the nature of his love for the flock.

1. Do I go out of my way to honor the elderly?

2. Do I equally value brothers who are both rich and poor?

3. Do I talk disparagingly about members of the Lord's flock to other pastors?

4. Do I willingly set aside my own rights to avoid being a stumbling block to weaker believers?

5. Do I rejoice in the success of members of the Lord's flock and share with other believers that success, ie., Announce weddings, baby births, engagements, promotions, etc.

6. Do I willingly listen to the least of my brethren.

7. Do I expect others to meet my standards of conduct and judge them when they don't?

8. Do I dedicate myself to "Catching people doing something right" rather than rejoicing when I catch them doing something wrong."

9. Do I positively reinforce members of the Lord's flock when they fail?

10. Do I display a grateful spirit and thank the Lord for His flock?

11. Do I go out of my way to communicate my love for the children in the Lord's flock?

12. Is my love for the flock evident enough so that people believe that I genuinely love them?

ON PEOPLE'S LOVE FOR THEIR PASTOR.

Many of the things that I have presented may not be true in the ministry of every pastor. In my case they have evolved over a period of 57 years of pastoral ministry. Laymen need to evaluate if their love for their pastor is genuine and how do they communicate this love?

1. Do I pray regularly for my pastor and the members of his family?

2. Do I encourage him if I observe a weakness in his ministry or do I criticize him to other members of the congregation?

3. Do I criticize my pastor or members of his family in front of my children not considering the consequence in their lives?

4. Do I encourage my pastor by sharing how the Lord used him in bringing blessing to my soul?

5. Do I have unrealistic expectations of his ministry?

6. Do I compare my pastor to other pastors not recognizing that each man is gifted differently.

7. Do I seek my pastor's success by being willing to help him where I can?

8. Do I express my love for my pastor with more than words?

9. Do I recognize that my pastor is a gift from God to the church?

Pastors can often feel unappreciated because people assume that their dedication of time and resources is something that is part of their "job." Often there is no gentle evaluation or consideration when the budget time comes and their needs are overlooked. Loving a pastor means that the flock is dedicated to supporting the pastor and his family not just "paying" him a salary. There are often abuses on both sides in this process but they should be discussed and a unity of purpose and process should be agreed upon.

ON THE CONSEQUENCE OF LEAVING YOUR FIRST LOVE

When the church at Ephesus received the stinging rebuke of the Lord, He called on the church to remember the relationship as it used to be and repent in order that it may serve with the intensity of love the Lord requires. Failure to do so meant that the Lord would take away His hand from the church and it would no longer be a part of the Lord's promise: *"I will build my Church"* - Matthew 16:18.

The consequence of defiling the Lord's church is brought home in Paul's commentary in 1 Corinthians 3. He discusses the ministry of laboring together with the Lord in a synergistic ministry. He uses the phrases "every man" and "any man" to identify those involved in building upon the foundation laid by the Lord Jesus. He warns the "builders" to take heed how they build. He pronounces that the church is the temple of God and warns if "any man" defiles the temple, him shall God destroy - 1 Corinthians 3:16-17. False teaching defiles the church. Sinful living defiles the church. A lazy pastor defiles the church. Angry pastors defile the church. Unqualified spiritual leadership defiles the church.

Many spiritual leaders do not finish well because their ministries have been destroyed by the disciplining hand of God. It has always been my prayer "Lord, enable me to finish well." Loving the Lord will all your heart, soul and body makes serving the Lord a privilege and not a burden. Ministry is not merely an endeavor to please the Lord but is an expression of the Lord's confidence in His child in allowing him to serve. Each believer has a particular place in God's plan and the Lord gives him the spiritual gifts to fulfill that ministry. Self-centeredness results in believers refusing or ignoring the service God plans for them so that they might order their lives according to their own priorities. The person that understands that he is not his own but has been bought with a price responds to the opportunity to serve with "Here am I lord, send me."

My Jesus I love Thee, I know thou art mine.

For Thee all the follies of sin I resign.

My gracious Redeemer, my Savior art Thou.

If ever I loved Thee, My Jesus 'Tis now.

CHAPTER ELEVEN

How Do I Maintain a Sense of Humor?

There are numerous incidents that take place around weddings. Many occur during the rehearsals but occasionally one takes place during the ceremony. One of my dear friends led in prayer at his grandson's wedding and on the way down the steps following his prayer, he tripped and did a complete flip landing on his back. The audience gasped but my friend, known for his sense of humor, picked himself up and declared "I did that better at rehearsal." The tension was broken and the wedding proceeded without interruption. But a memory was made and the wedding will always be known for my friend's quick wit. In my own experience, there have been a few weddings that stand out in my memory. At my first wedding, the bride was an hour and a half late. When we called to see if she was actually coming she assured us that she will get there as soon as possible. Then there was the bride that was so nervous that all she could do was giggle. Another bride came to the altar with long white gloves. I looked to see if they were "ring finger gloves." They were not, so I had to quietly ask her to remove the glove on her left hand so we could have a ring ceremony. I stuffed it in my pocket and continued with the ceremony. Once I neglected to include the vows in their rightful place and right before the announcement and the kiss I realized this so I announced that the vows were the most important thing in the wedding so they were to be exchanged last. Later a dear lady said: "Pastor you are so creative keeping the vows until last. It was so effective." I didn't confess to her that I had forgotten to administrate the vows in their place and placing them last was a quick thought to cover my mistake.

ON LAUGHING AT YOURSELF

A sense of humor is a must in the ministry. Many spiritual leaders take themselves far too seriously. Pastors make mistakes and sometimes these mistakes are very humorous. I remember one graduation at the Chapel Christian Academy when we had arranged for a photographer to be stationed down front to take a picture of each graduate as he/she received his/her diploma. We placed a note in the program requesting that those attending refrain from taking flash pictures. We were not into the program very far when flash-bulbs began to pop and it was evident that our request hadn't been noticed. I had to make a few announce-ments so I took the occasion to point out that flashes were very disrupting and that the school is going to provide copies of the main events in the graduation to the student as a gift. I noted that we had our own designated "flasher" down front. There was a deafen-ing silence followed by an eruption of laughter. When I realized what I had said, I also laughed and said, "Well so much for a dignified atmosphere!" I showed no embarrassment but simply was willing to laugh at myself.

ON DEALING WITH EMBARRASSMENT

It does no good to become irritated or mad when someone does something to embarrass you. When I was called to be the pastor at the Braintrim Baptist Church in Laceyville, Pennsylvania, I had just gradu-ated from seminary. The local paper came and inter-viewed me for an article announcing that the Baptist Church had called me to be its pastor. The day the paper came out I was a patient in the local hospital with a kidney infection and a nurse came into the room with a copy of the paper. She held it at arms length and said: "You might want to read this." There on the front page was my picture along with the article which included a paragraph reading: "Unmarried women of the congregation are requested to keep their distance from Pastor Gregory since he is married and wishes to remain free of sin and debauchery." I was aghast and immediately called my wife. She related that she had been up to the grocery store and there were people standing around reading the paper and involved in lively discussion.

When the editor saw the article he stopped the presses and removed the paragraph. He came to visit me and placed in the next issue a long apology. Apparently he had written this on the side of the article as a joke to his female linotype operator and she had included it in the article. My response to his visit was to say that my father was a newspaper man and I can understand how something like this can take place in the process of getting a paper to the press. I assured him that I held no ill will toward him even though many in the congregation were as mad as a wet hen and had cancelled their subscription to the paper. The article worked to my advantage, however, since I received the "sympathy" of the whole community. This gave me entrance into the lives of people that may have been beyond my reach under normal circumstances. Needless to say the church had exceptional coverage during the six years that I was its pastor.

One day I received a call from a man who was very ill asking me to come to see him. He was a life-long resident of Laceyville but never darkened the door of the church. I looked on the occasion as an opportunity to lead him to the Lord. When I arrived he said: "Pastor, I have something that I have to confess before I die." I had no idea what he was going to say and my mind began to play tricks on me with all kinds of scenarios. He called attention to an incident some 65 years before when someone sneaked into the church on Sunday afternoon when a baptism was scheduled for that night. The baptismal was lined with a gray lead which made it impossible to see the result of what he was about to do. He poured a bottle of blue dye into the waters so that when the baptism took place that night the blue dye did its job. No one ever found out who did this dastardly deed and it was to be unknown until he confessed to me that it was he. I laughed within myself at his creativity and tried to talk to him about his soul but to no avail. To this day I often wonder if he really wanted to be free from this deed or just wanted everyone to know that he did it.

One day my young son was playing in the church parking lot. As little boys will do, he was picking up stones and throwing them. One of the dear ladies of the church happened by and said: "Ricky, you better stop throwing those stone since you might break one of the stained glass windows." Ricky replied, "Its all right, my father owns this church!" Needless to say, he was corrected but I had to keep my sense of humor.

A sense of humor will keep one from being discouraged. We all remember our first funeral. The town drunk had passed away and the family asked me to officiate at his funeral. I was twenty-two years old and this was my first funeral. Needless to say I was a bit nervous. His two sons were pall bearers along with several of his drinking buddies. The sons, who were in jail at the time, were accompanied in handcuffs by Sheriff's Deputies only to be released to carry the casket. His drinking buddies were "under the influence" and staggered while attempting to place the casket in the hearse. I reflected on this experience and concluded that I had indeed started from the bottom and the only way from here is up.

I had other funeral experiences like that of a lady who asked to speak at her son's funeral. She insisted that people have an opportunity to speak also. When her turn came, she went on and on about what I thought was her son's nickname, only to find out later that she was talking about looking forward to going to heaven to see her dog!

Humor is not only something that you do, it is often something that happens to you. It keeps you from being irritated by people and events and enables you to laugh both at the events and at yourself. One of the classic illustrations of this happened when we were candidating at Limerick Chapel. Carol has a reputation in our family for her "spoonerisms." During the evening service she was asked to give a greeting. Being the sensitive lady that she is, she wanted to thank the church and especially our host. She said: "We want to thank all of you for your kind hospitalization." She turned to me and said: "Did I say hospitalization? I meant hospitality!" She began to laugh at herself and the congregation joined her. Later she was told that right then and there people knew they wanted this lady to be their pastor's wife.

CHAPTER TWELVE

How Do Experiences Help to Formulate Who You Are?

Little did I know when I was growing up that those things to which I was exposed and those things I experienced in my family were creating the person that would be a servant of the Most High God. I am reminded of an article on *Inspiration* by B.B. Warfield in the International Standard Bible Encyclopedia. In the article Warfield suggests that the writers of Scripture were products of the divine design, brought to pass by their experiences and heritage. He points out:

"There is to be considered the preparation of the men to write these books, a preparation, physical, intellectual, spiritual, which must have attended them throughout their whole lives, and indeed must have had its beginning in their remote ancestors, with the effect of which was to bring the right men to the right place at the right time, with the right endowments, impulses, acquirements, to write just the books that were designed for them Or consider how a psalmist would be prepared to put into moving verse a piece of normative religious experience: how he would be born with just the right quality of religious sensibility, of parents through whom he would receive just the right heredity bent, from whom he would get precisely the right religious example and training, of circumstances of life in which his religious tendencies should be developed precisely on the right lines; how he would be brought through just the right experiences to quicken him in the precise emotions he would be called upon to express, and finally would be placed precisely in the exigencies which would call out their expression." (Benjamin Warfield, *Inspiration,* Wm. B Erdmans, Grand Rapids, MI, in The International Standard Bible Encyclopedia – Volume III, 1956, pp 1480-81).

In the Apostle Paul's case, it is evident that his parents, his upbringing, his education, his training in the OT Scripture, his relationships and his zeal were involved in formulating the mind of the servant of God whose intellect, education and courage enabled him to be the conveyer of the Word of God and whose vision resulted in the expansion of the church from Jerusalem to Rome.

Eric Little, who was the focus of the film *Chariots of Fire,* realized this truth when he said: "God made me fast and He gets great pleasure when I run." Jeremiah's life message could be condensed into a few short words *"Before I formed you in the belly, I knew you, and before you came forth out of the womb I sanctified you and ordained you a prophet unto the nations"* - Jeremiah 1:5. Time and again in the Word of God there are illustrations of individuals designed by God and equipped to fulfill the ministry of God's choosing. Moses' experience in the household of Pharaoh and his sojourn in the back side of the desert molded him into the man God would use to deliver Israel from its bondage in Egypt. Time spent by Joseph in Potiphar's house and subsequently in prison under Pharaoh's wrath prepared him to be a leader in Egypt. Being equipped by the Holy Spirit makes one complete to do every good work having all the tools necessary to be and do that which is pleasing in His sight - Hebrews 13:21.

ON EMBRACING FAILURE

Some of the most important equipping experiences come through mistakes and failure. Learning from failure enables one to respond to experiences in ministry that do not "go your way." Sometimes when failures happen to other people they have an impact upon you. When I was in High School, baseball was my life. I remember one incident in my High School baseball career when we were behind in the bottom of the ninth by one run. We were at bat with two outs and I was on deck. The runner on third base took a long lead and in trying to get back, fell down. He was picked off, ending the game. I was so disgusted that I banged my bat on the ground and uttered a word that a Christian should avoid. I was deeply concerned about my testimony since I had just recently repented of my backsliding and had shared this with my class-mates. In reacting with disgust and anger, the flesh manifested itself. I was heartsick and I immediately fell to my knees acknowledging my sin and claimed the Lord's forgiveness. I learned that day that whenever you react to another's failures you open yourself up to being controlled by your weaknesses. Paul reminds the Galatian believers: *"Brethren, if a man be overtaken in a fault, you which are spiritual, restore such a one in the spirit of meekness; considering yourself, lest you also be tempted"* - Galatians 6:1.

Through the years I found that the failure of others provides an opportunity to love, understand and encourage my brother. I am sure all of us can realize that God often allows these failures to mold us into pastors who will feed the flock with knowledge and understanding - Jeremiah 3:15. It is difficult to comfort someone if you have never experienced the comforting ministry of the Holy Spirit yourself. I remember a conversation with my friend, Ed Smith of the Pocket Testament League. He shared how devastated he was when his wife passed away and how many of his friends tried to comfort him to no avail with the usual things that people say. However, a man came up to him and placing his arm around him, whispered in his ear "I know what you are going through, Ed, I lost my wife just last month." Ed shared that those words resonated in his soul and were the source of encouragement and peace. Paul reminds the Corinthian believes: *"Blessed be God, even the Father of our Lord Jesus Christ, the Father of mercies and the God of all comfort; who comforts us in all our tribulation, that we may be able to comfort them which are in any trouble, by the comfort wherewith we ourselves are comforted of God"* - 2 Corinthians 1:3-4.

One night I returned to the parsonage after a difficult congregational meeting where a man accosted me because I had shared that I had had the privilege of leading his teen-age son to the Lord. The man took great offense at my statement since he believed that his son had already been saved. No one came to my defense, even though there was no evidence that the young man knew the Lord. I was very discouraged by the incident and was wallowing in self pity when a knock came at the door. One of the young men in the church was there and said, "Pastor, I came to pray with you. I figured you could use some encouragement." I'll never forget what it meant to me to have that young man kneel with me at our living room couch and join me in pouring out our hearts to the Lord in behalf of that father and his son. I learned that night how important it was to be available to *"comfort the easily discouraged and support the spiritually weak."*

ON LEARNING LIFE'S LESSONS

Sometime the things we do impact another's life when we never intended them to do so. When I was a youngster, I had three older sisters that I felt "picked" on me and I often looked for opportunities to "get even." One such opportunity presented itself to me when we were climbing a tree at my uncle's home. My sister Joanne had climbed higher than I when a branch she was clinging to snapped and she plunged to the ground As she fell, she passed by me. I reached out with my foot and kicked her turning her right side up and she landed on her feet. Although shaken she was not injured. I thought by kicking her I was "getting even" but I was really helping her out. Genesis 50:20 says: *"As for you, you thought evil against me; but God meant it for good."* I learned that day that the Lord can take the expressions of our flesh and bring to pass good.

Losing one's temper can be devastating but it can also lead to the realization that this weakness needs the sanctifying power of the Holy Spirit to make the changes in our lives. Ephesians 4:31 challenges believers to *"allow all bitterness, and wrath, and anger, and clamor, and evil speaking, be put away (passive) from you with all malice: and be kind one to another, tenderhearted, forgiving one another, even as God for Christ's sake has forgiven you."* One day during a missions committee meeting there was a discussion concerning the upcoming recommendations it was to make to the budget committee. One of the members asked who was on the budget committee. I gave their names and one of the men on the missions committee "lost it." Throwing a book across the table he angrily declared that one of the individuals named to the budget committee should not be on that committee. His conclusion came as a result of unresolved issues from the past. When we left the meeting, I took the man aside and said that I wanted to talk to him before prayer meeting that next Wednesday night. When he came in, he humbly confessed that his reaction was inappropriate and said that he had sought out every member of the missions committee asking for their forgiveness. I then challenged him to address the strained relationship with the man that he was so opposed to serving

CHAPTER THIRTEEN

How Do I Do the Work of An Evangelist?

A part of the Apostle Paul's charge to Timothy was to *"do the work of an evangelist"* - 2 Timothy 4:5. This charge was in addition to *"preach the Word: be instant in season and out of season; reprove, rebuke, exhort with all longsuffering and doctrine"* - 2 Timothy 4:2. I think Paul realized that it is possible that one can be so involved in being discerning and guarding the truth that the saving truth of the gospel message will not be clearly presented which captivates the soul. I have been in churches where the teaching of the Word of God dominated the church's program, but both the spiritual leadership and the people were not involved in reaching men for Christ. I have also been in churches where it was believed that evangelism was the sole purpose of the church and very little good Bible teaching was present. It is incumbent upon a church's spiritual leadership to model the importance of soul winning as one of the three basic objectives in pursuit the church's purpose of glorifying God. A balanced church will have a vertical objective of the Exaltation of God in worship, a horizontal objective of Edification in developing body life and equipping God's people for the work of the ministry and an outreach objective in Evangelism through missions and personal witnessing. All of the activity of the church should be able to be classified under one of these three objectives.

ON THE BIBLICAL TASK OF EVANGELISM

I want to focus on the third objective, evangelism. One category of gifted men that the Lord gives to the church in Ephesians 4:11-12 is that of Evangelist. In today's church, an Evangelist is often identified as a man that goes from church to church holding special evangelistic campaigns. I am not sure that this is the primary meaning intended by the Apostle Paul in Ephesians. Paul writes to Timothy to *"do the work of an Evangelist"* - 2 Timothy 4:5. At the time, apparently Timothy was still in Ephesus equipping the saints. Doing the work of an evangelist does not seem to fit a gifted man going from church to church to hold special meetings. It might be more accurate to envision Timothy's ministry as an evangelist to be equipping the saints in the declaration of the Gospel in and through the local church in Ephesus. Paul is reminding Timothy to teach men to share their faith and to preach the gospel in the community in which they live. Although it is not wrong to see one of the functions of the evangelist to be a gifted man who is an itinerate preacher, I believe the local congregation should also envision a man gifted in evangelism as a member of the pastoral staff. Many congregations have men among their memberships that demonstrate this gift. They should be trained and encouraged to be a part of training others to "do the work of ministry" as evangelists. This would be the fulfillment of 2 Timothy 2:2: *"And the things that thou hast heard of me among many witnesses, the same commit thou to faithful men who will be able to teach others also."* The most effective evangelism is characterized by God's people being excited by the truth and power of the Gospel and, therefore, have a burden to share it with those who are lost. Trusting the "preacher" to be the only presenter of the Gospel is a misnomer and will result in a passive body of believers. A vibrant congregation of members involved in personal evangelism is evidence of a spiritually healthy body. Training people to do evangelism must include more than just methods. Matthew notes in Matthew 9:35-38 that Jesus left us an example of doing the work of an evangelist:

"And Jesus went about all the cities and villages, teaching in their synagogues, and preaching the gospel of the Kingdom, and healing every sickness and every disease among the people. But when He saw the multitudes, He was moved with compassion on them because they fainted and were scattered abroad as sheep having no shepherd. Then saith He unto His disciples, The harvest truly is plenteous, but the laborers are few. Pray ye, therefore, the Lord of the harvest, that He will send forth laborers into His harvest."

1. It was a life style
    a. Wherever Jesus went He was reaching out to people, teaching, preaching and meeting their personal needs.
    b. He was aware of the plight of the lost
        (1) He was moved with compassion
        (2) They were troubled and were thus scattered abroad
        (3) There was no shepherd to protect them, feed them and give them guidance
2. It was a life message
    a. There are souls everywhere waiting to hear the truth
    b. There are few who realize this and are willing to enter the harvest
3. It was a life challenge
    a. Plead with the One who is the Lord of the harvest
    b. To compel His children into the Harvest
        (1) Pray comes from a word often translated compel or beseech
        (2) Send comes from a word which means compel or cast out.

Peter shares with the believers in Asia Minor that *"Jesus left us an example that we should follow in His steps."* - 1 Peter 2:21. Although the verse's primary reference is to follow Jesus in His response to suffering, the principle can be used in other applications as well. Seeking to be Christ-like in one's burden for souls, faithfulness in prayer, clarity in message and influence on others should be the goal of every believer. It is for this reason that the Gospels are so important. Being familiar with the details of the life of Christ provides a reservoir of examples of how believers are to respond to life situations. A few years ago there was a wrist bracelet with the letters WWJD. The letters stood for WHAT WOULD JESUS DO. Many wore that bracelet having no idea what Jesus would do for they were not aware of the details of the life of Christ. There is a wonderful verse in Romans 8:28 which may be paraphrased: *"God is able to work together with all things, to bring to pass Christ likeness, in those who love God and are the called according to His purpose."* Christ-likeness includes more than responding to hardships. It also includes His passion for righteousness, His priority of pleasing the Father and loving His spiritual sons and daughters.

It is not considered politically correct to share the Gospel with people today since one's faith is considered to be intensely personal. Consequently, confrontational evangelism is not always the most productive.

Winning a person's trust and admiration by living a consistent Christian life opens the opportunity to share the reasons behind your confident and personal relationship with God. This approach is called lifestyle evangelism. It is only effective, however, if one determines that, when the occasion arises, the details of the Gospel will be shared and an invitation to trust Christ be issued. It should never be used, as it sometimes is, to escape the responsibility of sharing the Gospel. Other methods can be used such as distribution of tracts, beach evangelism, door to door calling as well as many other methods of spreading the Gospel. I have known people who came to Christ as a result of God using a diverse number of methods. But any method that is used should not violate clear biblical principles and needs to be covered by intense prayer that properly prepares the bearer and hearer of the Gospel. I have known people that become "pests" as they intensely push the gospel upon people. In such cases the "salvation prayer" is often repeated just to get rid of them.

It should be noted that the Lord prepares hearts to receive the Gospel and leads His servants to take advantage of His preparation. One Saturday night after spending all day driving our church bus home from Word of Life Island, a knock came at our door. There stood the town drunk. He told me that the young man that owned the local bar was in Robert Packer Hospital in Sayre, Pennsylvania about 50 miles away. He requested that I visit him and I assured him that I would do so on Monday. He grabbed me by the shirt and forcefully instructed me to do so that very evening. Something about his insistence made me realize that this visit was of utmost importance. I had a throbbing headache so I called one of our deacons and asked him to drive me to Sayre. When I walked into the man's room his wife and mother were there and they thanked me for coming but shared that Ed had slipped into a coma and was unresponsive. I walked over to the bed and taking him by the hand noticed that he was awake and responsive. I took out my Bible and shared the Gospel with him and then asked him several questions. Did he know that he is a sinner? Did he trust the Lord to keep His promises? Did he believe that Jesus had died on the cross to pay for his sin? Would he reach out in faith and trust the Lord Jesus Christ to be his Savior? Although he couldn't speak, he understood the questions and after each one I asked him to squeeze my hand if the answer was "yes." Tears began to run down his face as he realized that was now a member of God's family. I left Sayre that night thanking the Lord for using the town drunk to insist that I go *now*. Ed went out into eternity before I arrived home that night.

preach the Gospel to all nations. Since most churches cannot supervise and organize their missionaries, they choose as a partner a missionary organization with whom they are doctrinally and philosophically compatible. The missionary organization recognizes that the commissioning church is the sending agent and thus includes the church in major decisions as to the use of missionary talent, relocation and discipline when necessary. Thus the church must fulfill the responsibility of the sending church and delegate the authority to its Mission Partner to supervise and develop its missionaries. I am aware of one Mission Board that invites and pays for the pastor of a missionary candidate to attend candidate school with the candidate. During that time a firm partnership occurs in the training and use of the prospective missionary.

The aim of missionary evangelism must be to grow a self governing and sustaining local church which reflects its doctrine and philosophy. The Apostle Paul illustrates this principle in Acts 20:4: *"And there accompanied him into Asia, Sopater of Berea, and of the Thessalonians, Aristarchus and Secundus, and Gaius of Derbe, and Timotheus and of Asia, Tychicus and Trophimus."* These came from different local churches to become what some say was the first Missionary Organization. Learning to work together to accomplish a common goal is essential to successful missionary evangelism.

Just as in the text informing us of the churches sending men to work with the Apostle Paul, today's missionary activity and personnel illustrate the way in which like-minded churches can work together in synergistic ministry. The sum total in such ministries is greater than that of the sum of the individual parts. A mission board is the logical vehicle to accomplish this. Churches should become partners with mission boards that can enable the church to "go into all the world" and preach the Gospel to all people groups. It is my conclusion that mission boards exist to facilitate the church's commission to spread the Gospel. The authority to use a church's missionary comes through a church delegating that authority along with the corresponding responsibilities.

Synergistic evangelistic efforts have become popular among churches. Large evangelistic campaigns have been planned with thousands attending. Many churches become the sponsors of such campaigns. There are several potential problems with such an effort.

1. The sponsors can be so diverse that unbiblical alliances and denial of cardinal doctrines can be present leading some into ignoring the biblical doctrine of separation from unbelief.

2. Since there are many sponsoring churches, those coming forward to trust Christ as Savior must be sent back to the churches where they have not heard the Gospel.

3. The great fallacy of "the end justifies the means" is often employed to gain the widest exposure and thus reaching the maximum audience. The reasoning is employed by sincere believers that "if people are being saved, how can it be wrong."

After the wall came down there were many mass evangelism campaigns held in the former Soviet Union countries. It was the observation of the Christians in these countries that it had little or no lasting effect and made it harder to reach those exposed to these efforts.

ON PRAGMATISM IN EVANGELISM

Dr Bob Jones, Sr. often said: "It is never right to do wrong in order to get a chance to do right." There is always consequence to disobedience. Samuel once said: *"To obey is better than sacrifice."* When a church practices the principle of "the end justifies the means" it will soon depart from implementing its doctrinal statement in order to include people of a different doctrinal persuasion. In the *History of Princeton College and Seminary,* James Calhoun pointed out the demise of Princeton College began when professors that did not agree with the college's doctrinal positions were allowed to join the faculty as long as they did not teach in the Bible Department. Liberalism began its insidious infecting process thus destroying the foundation and rendering the college impotent in defending the Faith. I knew of one Bible Church that granted membership to a believer who was an Amillennialist even though its doctrinal statement was clearly pre-millennial and pre-tribulational. The man was very charismatic and soon was elected to the Board of Elders. The church's doctrinal statement became just a document with no lasting ability to preserve the purity of the church.

Evangelism, whether personal, lifestyle, confrontational, missionary, or campaign must first agree on the Gospel; secondly, must agree doctrinally; and, third must be local church based.

ON ECUMENISM IN EVANGELISM

A number of years ago when a great evangelistic campaign was attempting to reach the world for Christ by the year 2000, I received a call from a leading evangelical leader asking for our cooperation. I brought up the inclusion of Roman Catholics among the sponsors. He replied "If we are to preach the gospel to all the world by 2000, we are going to need the Catholics to help us." I replied: "with what gospel?" He reminded me that there were genuine believers in the Catholic Church. I observed, "That may be so, but they are bad Catholics since they are not subject to the church's ruling that all that trust in 'by faith alone in Christ alone' are to be considered Anathema." (Council of Trent)

Identifying the content and demands of the Gospel are critical to any evangelistic effort. Recently there has been controversy concerning the demands of the Gospel. All agree that *"by grace are you saved through faith and that not of yourselves, it is the gift of God, not of works, lest any man should boast"* - Ephesians 2;8-9. The question is debated as to whether saving faith is merely agreeing to "accept the Lord" or does the gift of saving faith come to those who call upon the Lord to save them out of genuine repentance. It is important that the various dimensions of grace be recognized. Paul in writing to Titus pointed out that *"for the grace of God that brings salvation has appeared to all men, teaching us that denying ungodliness and worldly lusts, we should live soberly, righteously and godly in this present world"* - Titus 2:11-12. Can we expect that when the Holy Spirit enables a person to change his mind concerning the offensiveness of his sin and trusting Christ as Savior that there will also be the discipline of grace that impacts how the new believer lives? There are those that postulate that one's justification does not guarantee ones participation in

CHAPTER FOURTEEN

How Do I Understand the Depth and Breadth of Ministry?

During my seminary years I took as many courses as possible from Dr Allan MacRae. He was a wise scholar and was able to make Church History come alive. Every once in awhile he would drop an observation on ministry. I remember one day he said: "Anyone worth half their weight can be busy in ministry 100% of the time. But that would not be wise. Learn how to say 'no.'"

Shortly after I came to Limerick Chapel we had a series of meetings with Dr Lehman Strauss. Each night he would wait for me to take him to his motel. I inherited from the former pastor the responsibility of turning out the lights and locking the many doors. The second night of the meetings, Dr Strauss who was patiently waiting for me, said, "Richard, what in the world are you doing? That should not be your responsibility. You are robbing your deacons of fulfilling their ministry." Sure enough at the next deacon's meeting I related my conversation and they willingly assumed the responsibility. I learned that night not to assume responsibility that others in the body can do.

ON SAYING "NO"

Through the years I have found saying "no" is very hard and takes thoughtful discernment. Does an opportunity need my gifts? Is it consistent with my ministry goals or would it detract? What would be my motivation for involving myself in this opportunity? I know of a young man in his first full time pastorate who was asked to serve on a mission board. After much prayer and seeking advice, he turned the opportunity down. His reason was that he had only been in his present ministry for about a year and felt that he could not afford the time to do a good job serving on the board and it would detract from his primary responsibility. I am sure that in the years to come, he will have much exposure to mission activity and missionaries. If the opportunity presents itself again, I am confident that he will desire to become involved in the mission enterprise on the board level.

ON STAYING FAITHFUL

When I graduated from college, I became the pastor of a small church in the resort area of Lake Hopatcong, New Jersey. During the winter there were about twenty people, including children. But during the summer that grew to a couple of hundred. I rejoiced in the opportunity to learn on the job. Because the church was so small, I found it necessary to work to support my family. One of the young ladies in the church was a schoolteacher and she suggested that I apply to teach school. Interestingly enough, there was a shortage of teachers and I was hired even though my degree was a BA in Philosophy. They promised me a helping teacher but she never showed up. I was on my own. For the next three years I taught fifth and then the sixth grade. During the spring of my third year, the superintendent called me into his office and said that he had a proposition for me. He said that the district would pay my salary, give me a raise and pay for me to go to Rutgers University during the next school year to earn a masters degree in administration. When I finished my degree I would be hired as the principal of the new middle school that was being built. Most would look at this as being a wonderful opportunity. I returned home and my wife began to rejoice in our apparent blessing. When I showed some hesitancy she asked me what I thought we should do? After a time of prayer and discussion, but with marital unity, we decided that I should turn it down and tell them that I would not be back the next year. When others asked "why," I shared with them that it did not fit our plan to go to seminary. If I took the job they wanted a five-year commitment. The Lord used this to motivate us to leave all and enroll in seminary. We were comfortable in our ministry at Hopatcong. We had the security of a teaching job enabling me to fulfill the responsibility to provide for my wife and two little children. Therefore the decision was not an easy one. It was one of the many times we stepped out on faith and cast ourselves on the mercies of the Lord to provide for us while following His leading. In fact during the first semester of seminary, Carol worked on Friday and Saturday nights as a waitress in a local Chinese restaurant and I worked selling cemetery property.

This was not the first time that I had to make a decision to turn down an opportunity in order to keep my eyes on my goal of becoming a pastor. I had an opportunity in my senior year in High School to sign a professional baseball contract. While in college one of the teachers at Juilliard also taught at our college. He said that if I so desired, he could get me a scholarship to study voice at Juilliard.

Again, I had to recognize good opportunities to be distractions and the Lord enabled me to walk away from them.

ON THE RIGHT FOUNDATION FOR MINISTRY

It is important that one realize that taking care of the depth of one's ministry is the foundation upon which the Lord established the breadth of our ministries. I believe this was so in my own experience. Carol and I envisioned that someday we might be able to shepherd a congregation of several hundred but we never dreamed that the Lord would use me as the pastor of a large eastern church at Limerick. In my early years at Limerick, I limited my mission board involvement to WEF Ministries later to become Biblical Ministries Worldwide. The General Director, Henry Heijermans invited me to join the board and through the years we became very close as friends and co-workers. I spent many hours traveling in Europe and in consultation prior to board meetings when I served as the board president. I was given the privilege of serving on the Biblical Ministries Worldwide board for 35 years.

Additionally, I served on the Founding Board of Biblical Seminary. Each opportunity was preceded by careful thought and analysis of the time required and how it would fit into my schedule and priorities.

Sometimes you have to make a decision to sever relationships if you can no longer agree with the direction an organization is taking. In consultation with my board of elders it was my decision to drop off the Biblical board. After coming to IFCA International as its Director, I was invited by Dr. Robert Provost to take a trip with him to minister to pastors in Russia. Later when he was appointed President of Slavic Gospel Association, I was asked to serve on its board. Such opportunities were demonstrations of my overall commitment to the Lord Jesus as He built His church.

Farthest from my mind was my involvement in ministry in the former Soviet Union. As a result of serving on the Slavic Gospel Association board, I made fourteen trips to countries of the former Soviet Union with my friend Robert Provost. I remember the first time I was scheduled to speak at a conference in Ukraine. As we flew over the vast expanse of ocean, I sat looking out the window pondering the opportunity. I turned and said to Carol: "Can you believe that a couple of kids from the mountains of Pennsylvania have been invited to speak at conferences in Ukraine and Russia?" I did so with a sense of unworthiness but with a sense of great responsibility.

As a result of that trip, we invited the missionary organizations of these countries to send us the names and pictures of church planters looking for support.

We posted scores of pictures on the wall at our Annual Convention and before the convention was over, all of the missionaries had been adopted for financial and prayer support. The result was almost 700 churches planted in Ukraine and Belarus in the next ten years. Later in meeting with the President of the Evangelical Union of Baptist Churches in Belarus, he related to Dr. Provost and me the heart wrenching condition of the widows in the former Soviet countries. I mentioned that my wife had a ministry to widows in America, founding and producing the magazine Chera Fellowship for those having lost a loved one. He asked me if he invited her would she come? Without asking my wife, I accepted the invitation to have her come to these countries to share with the women and widows how the Lord could use them. Later she visited Belarus and Russia conducting sessions with the women and widows which resulted in an ongoing ministry conducted by women of the churches. Her ministry proved to be of great encouragement and Carol regarded it as one of the highlights of her life.

I found that as I became more mature in ministry that the Lord began to broaden its influence. However, there were more opportunities than I could in good conscience accept. It was a decision, on my part, not to "lend my name" without significant involvement.

Many pastors are too busy in their own churches and thus neglect their own families. A good principle is "Do not do those things others can do and do those things you are called to do." A good biblical illustration of this is found in Acts 6:1-4: *"In those days when the number of disciples multiplied, there arose a murmuring of the Grecians against the Hebrews because their widows were neglected in the daily ministration. The twelve called the multitude of disciples to them and said, It is not reason that we should leave the Word of God to serve tables, wherefore, brethren, look you out among you seven men of honest report, full of the Holy Ghost and wisdom whom we may appoint to this business. But we will give ourselves continually to prayer and ministry of the Word."* Andrew Bonar addressed this in his book "The Barrenness of a Busy Life." Some pastors are so involved in administration that preaching becomes a necessity rather than primary in their ministries. I once heard a sermon on "The Tyranny of the Urgent." Feeding God's people with meat requires time, exegesis of the text, historical research, organization and careful presentation with effective illustrations of the truth. I once heard a seminary professor that reminded his students that God's children are sheep and not giraffes and therefore the "cookies" must be served on the bottom shelf. Preaching over the heads to God's people may sound intellectual to some but it is confusing to the majority. "What did the pastor preach on this morning?" "I don't really know, but it was really deep." The variety of ministry opportunities must never distract from the necessary time to properly feed and protect and counsel God's flock.

ON ESTABLISHING PRIORITIES

Finally, spiritual leadership needs to establish a ministry plan with its priorities and then make decisions concerning the church's ministry in the light of this plan. While I was in Grand Rapids with IFCA International, a local Bible institute found it necessary to close its doors. In the process of distributing its assets it offered the Christian radio station it owned to a large independent church. After due consideration, the church turned down the opportunity to operate a Christian radio station because it did not fit its ministry plan. Many people in a congregation will endeavor to involve their church in a variety of ministry opportunities. These opportunities may be worthy but the personnel required to pursue these opportunities can deplete the servant pool necessary to effectively conduct the ministry of the local church. The welfare of the local church must be primary in the decision making process. The light shines the farthest when it is kept bright at home.

God is not dependent upon any of His servants to accomplish His will. In His great sovereign power, He will bring to pass His plan. This is illustrated by the words of Mordecai to Esther in urging her to intercede for her people, the Jews. *"For if you altogether hold your peace at this time, then shall the enlargement and deliverance arise to the Jews from another place.... and who knoweth if you are come to the kingdom for such a time as this?"* However, it should be noted that the Lord gives spiritual gifts to His children and His design for these gifts is to provide gifted men and women for the benefit of the local church to accomplish its biblical mandate to bring glory to God through worship, equipping the saints, and evangelism. When a church member determines to use his gifts in a para-church organization, he should do so having received the blessing of the church's spiritual leadership.

One of the things that often deter the breadth of one's ministry is being subjected to intimidation. The intimation of coworkers or fellow ministers can render one enslaved to conform to others expectations. Being free to do what one believes is right demands that you do not seek approval of others. A servant of the Lord answers to the Lord and to those who are over him in the Lord. Often others impose their convictions on you based upon their understanding of proper conduct. When I was in the middle of seminary, a local Bible conference invited me to provide the music during one of its summer sessions. When one of my seminary professors heard of this he called me in to have a talk. He mentioned that the director of the Bible conference had fallen out of favor with the chairman of the Seminary board and that I should reconsider accepting the invitation. I felt very intimidated by this and consequently cancelled the engagement. I always felt disappointed with my decision and in later years established a close working relationship with the Bible conference and its director. Being free to follow the Holy Spirit's leading does not mean to disregard the impact of your decisions. It means that you make those decisions in the light of Scripture and your understanding of biblical relationships. It is wrong to make your decisions on the basis of what men will think or say about you. Being accepted by all men is a dangerous goal. Responding to that kind of intimidation robs a man of his self-respect, peace of mind, and soul.

CHAPTER FIFTEEN

How Do I Finish Well?

"*I* have fought a good fight, I have finished my course, I have kept the faith" 2 Timothy 4:7

According to the apostle's letter to Timothy, he recognized the end of a life of sacrifice and suffering for the sake of the gospel and the testimony of Jesus Christ was at hand. It was no tragedy for Paul since he had made it clear that: "*for me to live is Christ and to die is gain.*" - Philippians 1:21. It has always been a dilemma to me to see believers tenaciously hang onto life and even become bitter when faced with a terminal disease. An illustration of this can be seen in the life of Demas, Paul's fellow laborer in the gospel. "*Demas has forsaken me, having loved this present world and has departed unto Thessalonica.*" - 2 Timothy 4:10. The implication in this verse is that it was too dangerous to be associated with Paul and so he took his leave. It is a shame that Paul in his final words could not give Demas a good report. In contrast is the faithful ministry of Priscilla and Aquila. We see them first in Acts 18:1-4 where they provide a home for their fellow "tentmaker." They found themselves in Corinth because they had been expelled from Rome when Claudius had given an edict that all Jews must leave Rome. When Paul found it necessary to leave Corinth, they accompanied him as far as Ephesus. It is evident that they had been taught the Gospel of the grace of God for when they heard Apollos preaching in the synagogue, they recognized that his understanding of the Gospel was limited. They took him aside and successfully communicated to him the "way of God" more perfectly. It should be noted that Apollos did not reject their counsel and Aquila and Priscilla were not hesitant to give it. It is an example of the unity of the Spirit. They appear again in Paul's narrative in Romans 16:3-5 where they are back in Rome and are regarded by Paul as *"my helpers in the gospel. Who have for my life laid down their own necks, unto whom not only I give thanks, but also all the churches of the Gentiles."* They have opened up their home again, and there is a church meeting in their house. They have a place in their hearts for the believers at Corinth for Paul in expressing thanks again in 1 Corinthians 16:19 said: *"The churches of Asia salute you. Aquila and Priscilla salute you much in the Lord with the church that is in their house."* They are still faithful as Paul gives

Our decision to move from Byron Center to a home in Florida was met with objection by our fourteen year old grandson. He came to see me and asked me to biblically justify retirement. I shared that in the Old Testament priesthood there were age limitations on a priest's active service; but, that didn't mean that he ceased to be a priest (Numbers 8:24-26). This did not seem to satisfy him and he continued to have a hard time with our leaving Byron Center and moving to Florida. I tried to communicate to him that I was not retiring but was *refocusing.* I would continue to preach and serve the Lord in whatever capacity the Lord provided for me. The community in Florida where we moved had a Bible class that was founded and taught by a man who served as a deacon in the Evangelical Free church in Fullerton, California. We attended the class for about a year. Later, he came to visit us and shared that he had the beginning stages of Alzheimer's disease. He shared that he had been praying that the Lord would provide someone to teach the class. It did not take long for us to respond that we would be glad to take on this ministry. Carol and I worked together to build this class and to begin to minister to people in our development who did not attend church any-where. We began a Sunrise Service at 7:00 am Easter Sunday morning with as many as 300 attending. We became members of Faith Baptist Church in Winter

Haven, joined the choir, and became a substitute adult Sunday school teacher. Preaching opportunities were many and I was invited to supply the pulpit of a church in Leesburg, Florida which I did for almost a year.

ON BEING WILLING

It was communion Sunday at Faith Baptist Church and I sat there with the elements in my hand. I was overcome by a feeling of uneasiness. I examined my heart for any un-confessed sin that would cause the uneasiness, but could not put my finger on anything. I softly prayed, "Father, I do not know what you are doing here, but whatever you want to do with me, it is OK." Immediately the uneasiness went away and was replaced with a warm calmness. The following Tuesday, I received a call from an elder at Grace Bible Church in Fair Oaks, California. He related to me the problems the church was having in the light of the church's discipline of its pastor. A split had taken place and I had been recommended to them as a possible interim pastor to help in the church's healing process. The Lord had prepared me for this while going through a disciplining process some 30 years before. I told him I would pray about it and talk with my wife. When I got off the phone, Carol said, "Who was that?" When I shared with her what we were being asked to do, I expected her to react negatively since our youngest daughter and her family had just moved to a school ministry in Bartow, Florida. I had related to her my experience the previous Sunday during the communion service. In the light of that she replied: "If that is what the Lord wants, we should do it!" I called the elder back and said that we would be willing to come out and visit with the church and elders. He agreed and said "can you come this weekend?" I replied, "At this short notice, tickets will be very expensive." His response was "When a patient is on the operating table, he needs a surgeon right away." We flew to Sacramento on Friday and had a series of meetings over the weekend. We found hurting elders, split families and a staff that was discouraged. We agreed to come and two weeks later we arrived as the church's interim pastor. The five months that we were there proved to be a special time as we shepherded people through times of discouragement, depression, anger and potential bitterness. When we left we felt like we were once again leaving family. We had helped the church to prepare to call a new pastor which they eventually did with a 100% agreement.

I found that I was very busy in my "retirement." I continued to preach, serve on the boards of BMW and SGA, serve a term as President of the Florida Regional of IFCA International, travel to conferences in Russia,

Ukraine, Belarus, France, Germany, the Netherlands and Israel.

One of the highlights of my retirement was co-authoring the book *On the Level* with my son, Dr. Richard W. Gregory. The book provides believers with the understanding that there are varying levels of relationships within the Body of Christ. It constructs a Pyramid of Responsibility of biblically mandated relationships and their uniqueness in the pursuit of obeying the Word of God in one's cooperative alliances. I am gratified to see the number of Christian colleges that have indicated that it is a must read and have included it in their curricula.

It has always been the goal of Carol and me to finish well. It was a regular part of our prayer life. Many times during my sermons I would point out that my greatest desire was to hear the Lord say to me: *"Well done my good and faithful servant, ... enter into the joy of thy Lord."* - Matthew 25:23. It was a constant reminder through the years that it is possible to serve the Lord admirably and then in the final stages of ministry to become careless and completely fail. Unfortunately your failure will be your legacy. Men who began well were slowly changed by their experiences, doctrinal challenges and desire to be relevant. Pride, jealousy, critical spirit, rejoicing in iniquity and struggling for control are among other self-centered pursuits that can contribute to a man's demise. Paul warned of this in 1 Corinthians 9:26-27: *"I therefore so run not as uncertainly; so fight I not as one who beateth the air; But I keep under my body and bring it into subjection; lest that by any means, when I have preached to others, I myself should be a castaway."*

When we were married in June of 1956, we adopted as our life verse Romans 8:28: *"And we know that all things work together for good to them that love God, to them who are the called according to His purpose."* We knew that this verse did not guarantee that the events of our lives would always appear to be "good for us," but we understood that God was able to work with all things in our lives in order to bring to pass the "good," that is, conforming us to the Lord Jesus Christ. What we claimed that day was God's ability to work in us and through us to model Christ-likeness. He taught us, through our failures, to respond and not react. Those lessons were not always easy. It is a comforting truth to realize that God's grace is always at work in us, disciplining us to *" deny ungodliness and worldly lusts, we should live soberly, righteously and godly in this present evil world."* - Titus 2 12. I can't remember how many times through the years we repeated the promise of Romans 8:28.

I have endeavored to write Ministry Matters at the urging of my colleagues, wife and children. When I was told that I had a terminal disease and my life expectancy was six months to a year, I knew I had to get at this right away. The prayers of God's people have sustained me and strengthen me through this process. All my life I have tried to teach people how to live, and now by God's grace I want to show them how to die. The peace I possess has been an enigma to my doctors and Hospice nurse. They observe the reality that by God's grace death holds no fears for me because *"For me to live is Christ, and to die is gain."* From the first days of being a new creature in Christ, I have looked forward to the day that I see my Master and Lord, Jesus Christ. I've sought to see Him glorified through my life as God's Spirit has continued to do the work of perfecting the image of Christ in me to which I have been predestined. I have had great joy in seeing the hand of God working in my life through various acquaintances, friends, colleagues, family members, church members, and at times, even strangers. I have had too many failures in my life to boast of myself. But I am able to boast of Christ in me, the hope of glory!

The apostle Paul set an example that has served throughout the years as an "enviable" terminus to life. Early in my ministry, I looked forward to what the end would bring if Jesus did not return for His church during my lifetime. I realized that in order to finish well, I would have to live every day as if it were a "finishing day," realizing that any day could be the day that I saw the Lord.

I have aspired to on that day say what Paul said: *"I have fought a good fight, I have finished my course, I have kept the faith."* Because of the faithfulness of God, a man is able to "make it" – being saved to the uttermost. Knowing this, Carol and I claimed as our life song "Great is Thy Faithfulness." The song testifies to the unchangeable nature of God's compassion and provision throughout the seasons of life. It declares that the heavens and all nature are witnesses of the manifold faithfulness of God in His mercy and love. It provides the comfort that God is faithful to pardon our sin, provide an enduring peace and assures us of His promised presence. Strength, hope and blessing become the products of our confidence in His faithfulness. The chorus extols the fact that God is continually teaching us anew each morning the breath of His mercies as He provides for our genuine needs. The truths expressed in this song have been the source of great joy in our walk through our seasons of life. It will be the song that we sing throughout eternity – to the praise of God the Father, to the glory of the Son of God, and in the power of the Holy Spirit. To Him be glory and praise forever!